OTHER PEOPLE'S
CHILDREN

BY

ANNA JUDGE VETERS LEVY

JUDGE, FIRST CITY COURT
NEW ORLEANS

THE RONALD PRESS COMPANY · NEW YORK

HV
9069
.L43

Library of Congress Catalog Card Number: 56–11293

PRINTED IN THE UNITED STATES OF AMERICA

PREFACE

In spite of all that has been said and written on the subject of juvenile delinquency, there is little understanding of the problems of the children who are called juvenile delinquents. Lurid headlines and sensational newspaper accounts play up the superficial aspects of the subject, while the real story of what goes on in the hearts and minds of youthful offenders remains untold.

Of the thirty thousand children who appeared before me during the time I served as judge of a juvenile court, there were very few whose stories, if they were but known in their entirety, would not touch the heart.

Perhaps these are other people's children, not yours or mine, or even our neighbors'. But the time has passed when we can ignore their troubles. Just as we now know that smallpox in the slums constitutes a danger to the homes in our garden districts, so do we also know that human failure, whether it be in high places or hovels, affects us, our families, our communities, and ultimately the nation.

The child who is deprived of all that children most need grows up to become the maladjusted adult who is a burden upon society and a threat to the lives and happiness of law-abiding citizens. We are responsible for this

iii

child. First of all, we are responsible to him for the conditions which have made him what he is, and we are also
responsible for him to our own children and to our children's children.

If this child comes into conflict with the law while he
is still a child, it is our duty to see that he gets justice—
not the narrow justice of retribution and vengeance, but
justice transcending the punitive and supplying the child
with understanding support and helpful discipline which
are usually the prerogatives of responsible parents.

This was the type of justice which was referred to by
a magistrate in New York who had to condemn four boys
to the electric chair. Their average age was less than
twenty years and, as the judge looked at them, he was
probably thinking that they should be standing on the
threshold of life with the bright promise which it holds
for other young people, instead of standing there before
him waiting to be sentenced to oblivion. The jury had
found them "guilty as charged," and the judge's sole function had become the pronouncement of the death sentence. But he took occasion to denounce society for the
injustice of having failed to help these youths while they
were still young and plastic enough to be amenable to
correction.

It should not be difficult to answer the question with
which the judge concluded his remarks: "When the young
human astray comes in contact with human justice for
the first time at the electric chair, who is the offender—
the young derelict, or he who might have devised and
applied a corrective, but did not?"

We are not informed as to how the parents of the victims of these young murderers felt, but we do know about
a father and mother whose only son was killed by a youth-

ful murderer and who were thereby shocked into a realization of their responsibility for what had happened. In the deepest sorrow that can come to a father or a mother, they wrote to the governor of the state and asked for executive clemency for the murderer of their son:

"We feel that this young murderer is the product of our system of society, for which all of us, and particularly persons in our position, are to some extent responsible. His father and mother are good, hard-working people. With them the struggle for existence was too bitter and exacting to permit them to devote the time and personal care necessary to develop the good and repress the evil in their son, who thus grew up amid the malign influences that surround the children of the poor in a large city."

There are few people who have not recognized some children as destined to become criminals if something isn't done to teach them to control their behavior. It was my responsibility to see some thirty thousand such children during my eight years on the bench of a juvenile court. And although the court over which I presided was ill-equipped with staff and facilities, we may have made up for these deficiencies in some measure by sincere interest in each child and genuine concern for his welfare. We also considered it part of our duty to try to secure for the court the equipment necessary to give children the advantage of all that is being learned and developed in the field of human behavior. If our progress in this respect was slow and painful, it may have been due to the many other worthy causes which cry out for public support and to the fact that the great-hearted American public responds more readily to the appeal of an individual child than it does to a plea on behalf of unknown thousands.

My regret is that I cannot tell you about more of the children whose cases I heard and studied, for I know that their stories would be equally moving. The cases which I have selected were chosen, not because they are more appealing than the others, but because they give a representative sampling of the children who appear before the juvenile courts of our country.

Anna Judge Veters Levy

New Orleans
July, 1956

CONTENTS

OTHER PEOPLE'S
CHILDREN

1

THE LONELY BROTHERS

When we saw the case of Thomas and Charles Doe on our docket, we sighed, "Running away again." These two very likable youngsters had been the cause of much concern to us because we feared that they would get into serious trouble before any satisfactory placement plans for them could be worked out. Having no placement facilities of our own, we had to depend upon public and private social agencies, which told us frankly that they gave preference to cases originating with them.

Tommy and Charlie had been brought directly to the Court by the police, who had found them in a third-floor-back apartment of the French Quarter, where they had been living with their mother and where they had continued to live for two years after her death. Tommy was eleven years old and Charlie was a little over thirteen. A medical check-up showed them to be in good health and of average size and weight. Tommy was light in coloring, and his merry blue eyes and quick smile won friends for him wherever he went. Charlie was brunet, with clear-cut features and big brown eyes which looked very sad when he told us how sorry he was about having run away again.

Neither of the boys knew anything about their father, except that he left before Tommy was born. Their mother had evidently not realized how ill she was, because she had never told them what to do when she "went away." (We never did succeed in locating any relatives.) Their own idea was that they should be allowed to go on living in the apartment; they were sure that they could take care of themselves. We talked to them about both institutional and foster home placement, but they were not enthusiastic about either.

We succeeded in having them accepted on an "emergency basis" in what was recognized as the outstanding institution of its type in the South. The placement was temporary, we were informed, and we would have to remove the boys whenever requested to do so. Having no alternative, we accepted these conditions. Within three days we were called upon to remove them. In spite of the swimming pool, the fine gymnasium, and numerous other advantages, the boys didn't like the institution, and they ran away at the first opportunity. They didn't run very far before they were apprehended by the police and brought back to the institution, but it was the policy of the institution not to keep any child who ran away or attempted to run away.

We requested the institution to give them another chance. They agreed to do so, provided we called the boys into Court and told them there was to be no more running away. After we had talked to the boys long and seriously, they promised not to run away again.

As far as we knew, they had kept their promise for

three whole weeks, but their names on the docket indicated that they must have run away again and that the institution was surrendering them to us.

Knowing we would have to find immediate placement for them, we looked over the file to ascertain if any of our requests for foster home placement for these boys had produced results. We saw what we expected to see: none of the agencies could give us any hope of being able to secure placement for these boys, either immediately or at any time in the near future. Often we had been told—and we knew it to be a fact—that the agencies were finding it increasingly difficult to secure good foster homes for children of any age, and it was almost impossible to find homes that were willing to accept adolescent boys. We also knew that although the agencies agreed with us about the desirability of keeping children from the same family together, they usually found it advisable to separate them for foster home placement. Experience had shown that brothers and sisters frequently combined in opposing and criticizing everything that foster parents tried to do for them. The agencies did not wish to jeopardize their program by destroying their relations with foster parents. They therefore asked us not to request that children be placed together.

In this case we had pointed out that all that Tommy and Charlie had to hold on to was each other, and we had advised the agencies that we could not consent to separating them. And so there were three strikes against these boys: they were adolescents, we wanted them placed together, and they had established a pattern of running away. We had every reason to be prepared for the agencies' unanimous decision that foster home placement was impossible for these boys.

As they came in, Tommy was talking to our Probation Officer, and he flashed a bright smile at the Court as he said, "Good morning, Judge." Charlie joined in the greeting, but he appeared more disturbed than we had ever seen him. He kept looking over his shoulder. When our eyes followed the direction of his glance, we saw two men standing by the door, one dressed in the uniform of a railroad Pullman conductor and the other in the work clothes of a farmer. We couldn't understand why the Probation Officer would want to bring in witnesses to testify that the boys had run away. That was a fact easily established by the testimony of the representative of the institution. Furthermore, the Probation Officer well knew that we were far more concerned about what we were going to do with these boys than we were about verifying the fact that they had run away again.

When the worker from the institution came in that morning to surrender custody of Thomas and Charles, she was surprised to see the boys. She had not expected to be able to surrender them physically. They had been missing from the institution for five days, and the worker didn't know they had been found.

As we soon learned, they had arrived in the city only an hour before, and their appearance in court at the moment their case was being called was a coincidence. The Probation Officer placed in front of us the folder containing the case history and all the other information about the boys and addressed the Court. "Of course your Honor remembers Tommy and Charlie." We looked at the boys and said that we were sorry that they were reported to have run away again. We said it as lightly as we could, because although we were worried about the boys, we didn't want to give them the impression that we thought too badly of them for having run away from a place in which they were unhappy. The Probation Officer started to say that, according to what he had heard just a few moments before, he was afraid it was something more serious than running away this time, but he was interrupted by the man who looked like a farmer. "I'll say it's something serious. It's robbery and assault and battery and arson. That's what it is, and I demand that these here kids get what's coming to them."

We let each of the witnesses say what he had on his mind, and in doing so they revealed not only their version of what had happened but also a great deal about themselves. The farmer, whose name was James Smith, had been driven to do the work of a man while he was still a child, and that was probably what had hardened him into a brutal and callous individual, totally devoid of human kindness. The Pullman conductor, Thomas Waters, referred to his childhood as a very happy time of his life. Everything he said indicated his concern and sympathy for the boys. After they completed their testimony, we told them that we wanted to hear the whole story from the boys and asked them not to interrupt.

Then we turned to the boys and explained to them that they didn't have to tell us anything if they didn't want to. We tried to reassure them and put them at ease by giving a little talk about the Constitution and the way it protected their rights. We felt sure that they understood enough of what we said to make them realize that the Court recognized that they had certain rights and that it was the Court's duty to protect these rights. We told them we knew that they weren't afraid of the Court and that we were depending upon them to speak the truth if they decided to say anything at all.

The boys looked at each other and then at the Court, and Charlie said they wanted to tell us all about it because they knew we would believe them. With the directness of youth, he aimed his first words at what he believed might be prejudicing them in the mind of the Court. "We know we didn't have any business running away from the Home again; and, honest, we really meant it when we promised not to do it again." Then he went on to explain that they didn't know how hard it was going to be to keep the promise when they made it. They didn't know that everyone in the place was going to be "down on them" for having run away the first time or that the other boys were going to be forbidden to play with them. They didn't know, either, that a nice lady would visit the Home and pick them out from all the other boys and ask them to show her around the place. Nor did they know that the lady would give each of them a new dollar bill when she was leaving.

Tommy filled in a pause in Charlie's account at this point by getting something off his mind. "It wasn't the money, Judge, it was just that she seemed to like us, and somehow that made us more lonesome after she was gone."

Charlie went on to tell how Tommy had given him his dollar and how he had rolled up both bills and hidden them in his undershirt. He said he knew they were breaking the rules when he did this because, "You're supposed to turn in anything you get, so they can keep it for you. But when you do that, it don't seem like it's yours any more." He looked us straight in the eye as he said he hoped we'd believe that they had no idea of running away when he hid the money, and we shouldn't blame the lady because she didn't even know that they were "run-away boys."

They carried the money around with them a whole week deciding they would turn it in the day before the big picnic. That way they could get it back again the next day to spend at the picnic. They still had the money, when they were told that they couldn't go to the picnic because they were "run-away boys." So they kept the money, playing with it while the other boys were away at the picnic. They had fun pretending they were spending the money for different things. When Tommy said, "Let's pretend we're buying bus tickets to a far place," it gave Charlie the idea that if they ran away they would have money to go somewhere this time.

They waited until the boys came back from the picnic. Amid the commotion nobody paid any attention to them. Although they knew where the bus station was, it took them a long time to get there. They could have taken the street car, but they wanted to save their money to buy tickets to a "far place."

In the waiting room they saw a long line of people waiting in front of the ticket window. They were just about to take their place at the end of the line, when Tommy spied a policeman. He nudged Charlie, and they pushed their way through the crowd to the opposite side of the room. Flattening their bodies against the wall behind the telephone booth, they watched the hands of the big clock tick off the seconds and the minutes of three hours. Then they heard the loud-speaker announce that there would be no more departures that night.

The policeman came in and looked around the room as the last stragglers were leaving. The boys were sure that he saw them and that he started to walk in their direction, but then he held up his arm and looked at his watch, turned on his heel, and left.

Tommy asked Charlie what they were going to do. Charlie said they'd better try to get a train at the railroad station. They started to walk along Canal Street, but they felt too conspicuous on the brightly lighted thoroughfare —almost entirely deserted because of the lateness of the hour. They knew they were easily identified by the khaki uniforms of the Home, and so they crossed over to an unfamiliar back street, which led them toward the railroad yards, instead of to the station.

Before they knew where they were, they found themselves in a maze of dimly lighted tracks, with engines shunting cars backward and forward all around them. They saw men rushing around with flashlights in their hands, but they couldn't get close enough to any of them to ask their way to the station. It was all they could do to keep from being knocked down by the locomotives which seemed to be coming at them from all directions. Tommy stumbled on one of the tracks, and Charlie pulled him off just in time to escape the switching engine which was bearing down on him.

The boys said it was a nightmare. They couldn't get out of the way of one locomotive without stepping into the path of another. They were almost exhausted, when an engine deposited a car directly in front of them and then puffed off. The big wooden door of the car was pushed back, and a man appeared in the opening. He was standing there looking down at the boys, with a lighted lantern in his hand, when Tommy called to him. "Mister, can you tell us how to get out of all these tracks? We're trying to find our way to the railroad station."

The noise made by the engines and the coupling and uncoupling of cars was almost deafening, and the man didn't seem to be able to hear them. He jumped to the ground and held the lantern up to Charlie's face and asked him what he wanted. Charlie repeated Tommy's question. "Do you know how we can get out of here?" The man shrugged his shoulders and scratched his head. "I sure don't. I'm just waiting for them to hitch my cattle car onto another train."

He noticed the boys were peering into the car trying to see the cattle, and he asked, "Know anything about cattle?" Tommy's reply came quickly. "No, we don't. But we're going to be cowboys when we grow up." The man took another look at Charlie before he said, "You look like a husky kid. How'd you like to get a free ride and make a few bucks besides, helping me with them cows?" The boys hesitated, and the man went on talking about how "dog tired" he was from four days on the road with the cattle and nobody to give him a hand. But when Charlie asked, "Will you take my brother, too?" he looked at Tommy and gruffly answered, "No." He let them walk a "good ways" down the track before he called to them, "O.K. Come on, both of you."

He told the boys to get in the car. Then he went off, leaving them to climb in as best they could. Charlie got in first, but when he saw that Tommy couldn't make it, he jumped down and helped him and then again pulled himself up into the car. It was so dark that they could hardly see the cows in the car, but they could hear "a whole lot of them" moving around, and they could smell them, too. When the man came back with the lantern, the boys saw that the cows had long horns and that they were tied very close together.

The boys were interested in the cows and started asking a lot of questions. If the man heard them, he didn't bother to answer. He hung the lantern on a hook in the ceiling of the car and showed the boys where the feed and water were kept. He handed each of them two buckets and told them to give a bucket of feed and two buckets of water to each cow. Then he lay down on a pile of hay and was snoring loudly when the car began to roll.

Some of the cows lost their balance at the first jerk of the train, and this caused a whole row of them to fall over on top of each other. One of them broke its halter and started a rampage, horning the other cows and knocking the buckets of feed out of the boys' hands. Tommy and Charlie were so frightened that they ran to the man and woke him up. He was very angry and cursed and swore at them so much that they were almost more afraid of him than they were of the cows.

At this point in Charlie's narrative, Tommy pointed to the farmer and said, "That's him, that's the man, and he knows that everything Charlie is telling is true. He did ask us to go with him and help with the cows, and he did tell us to get in the car. He wasn't telling the truth when he said we sneaked in the car when he wasn't looking."

We asked Charlie if he knew the man's name, and he said the man told them to call him "Mr. Smith," and one of the men who opened up the car at the end of the trip had called him "Jim Smith." But Charlie continued to refer to Mr. Smith as "the man" throughout most of his narration.

The boys were surprised at how easily the man got the cows back into place. He tied them up again and went back to sleep on the hay pile. The boys did their best with the feeding, holding tightly to the buckets when the cows tried to horn them out of their hands. Even so, a great deal of feed was spilled on the floor of the car, and when the thirsty cows saw them coming with buckets of water, they knocked them out of their hands. The floor was a slippery mass of feed and water, and the boys were soaking wet from head to foot by the time they had finished.

They didn't dare lie down on the hay alongside Mr. Smith, so they picked the only other dry spot in the car, which was on top of the sacks of feed. They were so tired that they could almost have slept standing up, and they didn't awaken until Smith dragged them down off the feed sacks, giving each of them a hard kick where it hurt most. Tommy screamed with pain, and Charlie could hardly hold back the tears, although he knew that he was too big to cry. Smith swore at them and used even worse language than when the cows had broken loose. He told them that he hoped that "that," meaning the kick, would teach them not to waste good feed and water.

It didn't teach them anything, except to be so afraid of Smith that they let him drive them and work them to the point of exhaustion. The cows had to be fed and watered twice a day, and once a day the boys had to squeeze in between the big animals to shovel up the ma-nure. Each shovel-full had to be carried to the end of the car and thrown into a high box.

Smith made a big pot of strong coffee every morning, and the boys drank as much of it as he would let them have. The bread he gave them was so hard and dry that they could hardly swallow it, so they "mostly lived on coffee."

Except for two streaks of light, which came in through wide cracks in the planks, the car was as dark in the day-time as it was at night. The boys lost count of the days; they were afraid to ask Smith how long it would take to get where they were going.

The train stopped many times, but the boys couldn't see out, and they never knew whether they were in a station or sidetracked in the woods. Mr. Smith got out of the car and locked the boys in whenever they were on a siding for any length of time. He never failed to come back before the train started, but he usually smelled of whiskey and treated them worse than before.

The boys didn't remember how many times they had fed and watered the cows and cleaned up the car, before they awoke one night and heard Smith talking to some men at the door of the car. One of the men flashed a light around the car and asked, "What've we got here?" Smith answered, "Forty-two head of cattle" and handed them some papers. He talked to them about how long the trip had taken and how often the train had been side-tracked. The men told him that his boy had been wait-ing every day and would be back with his truck in the morning. Smith called to them as they were leaving. "I've got two boys here, run-aways from New Orleans. I'll need them to help me unload these cows, and then I'll turn them over to the sheriff."

Tommy and Charlie lay down again and gave no sign of having heard what was said. Smith closed the door and took the lighted lantern off the hook and put it on the floor alongside the hay pile that served as his bed. He glanced in the direction of the boys. It was so dark in their corner that he couldn't have seen them even if they'd been sitting up. As a matter of fact, they were lying down, but they were watching every move he made. He walked around the lantern, and then sat down on the hay with his back to them. Charlie knelt upon the feed pile and strained his neck until he could see what Smith was doing. He was counting money, "a big roll of it," and after he had counted it several times, he went over to where his coat was hanging on the wall and put the money in the inside pocket. Then he lay down and went to sleep, without putting the lantern back on the hook. It wasn't very long before he was giving out the loud snores which meant that he was sound asleep.

Without a word, Charlie slid quietly to the floor and then helped Tommy to get down. They crept over to the door as quietly as they could and tried to open it without making any noise. But it was a heavy door, and the rail along which they had to slide it was very rusty. They kept pushing as hard as they could, and they had just succeeded in getting it open a few inches when Smith woke up.

He jumped up and grabbed both of them before they knew it. They tried to pull away from him and get back to the door, but he twisted their arms back of them. When he made the mistake of trying to hold both of them with one hand while he reached for a rope, Tommy managed to wiggle out of his grasp. He made a dash for the door, with Smith coming after him, still holding on to Charlie. Tommy would have been caught again if he hadn't ducked into the hay pile. He was trying for the door again, when Smith gave him a swift kick, which sent Tommy sprawling on the floor. He stretched out his hands to try to save himself, and one of his arms struck the lantern and turned it over. In a few moments the hay pile was in flames, and Smith let go of Charlie to run to the other end of the car for water.

The boys knew this was their only chance, and they took it. They pushed the car door open just enough for them to get through and jumped to the ground. They ran towards the railroad station, yelling, "Help, Fire." When they saw there was no one to hear them, they crossed over to some buildings on the other side of the tracks. Finding everything there tightly closed, they ran back to the tracks to signal some workmen who were coming along on a handcar. They shouted, "Fire," and tried to wave the car down, only to have the workmen laugh and wave back at them. They watched the hand-car, thinking that the men might notice the cattle car as they passed it. When they kept right on going, the boys decided that it was up to them to go back and try to help save those "poor cows" from being burned to death.

As they were walking along the tracks, Charlie suddenly felt "something like vibration" and turned around. It was the bright headlight of an approaching train. He pulled Tommy off the track and waited while the engine and several coaches went slowly past them. Then the train stopped, and a conductor and one passenger got out.

Charles hesitated before going on with his story. He looked at the Pullman conductor and said, "That's the conductor. He already told you what happened after that, and what he said was true. Do you want me to tell it again?"

Mr. Waters, who had been listening attentively, said, "I certainly wouldn't have wanted to tell anything but the truth about these boys, because I liked them from the very beginning. But I did get the wrong slant on them after I talked to Mr. Smith. Maybe it would be better if the Court let them tell the rest of their story."

Charlie went on to tell how they ran up to the conductor and told him that a car was on fire on the other side of the train. The conductor looked in the direction they indicated and couldn't see anything. Then he looked at them. They were dirty, and their clothes were torn and ragged. To the conductor they looked like the mischievous kids who are always hanging around railroad stations. He tried to chase them away, and then he walked up to the front of the train to talk to the engineer. Charlie thought he was going to do something about the fire, and so he called his brother. "It's all right, Tommy. Let's get on the train."

They went up the steps and through the open door of the Pullman car. Inside, all they could see were curtains hanging down, and they could hear that there were people sleeping behind the curtains. They saw the conductor come up the steps when the train started, and when he went into the car in front of them, they followed him until he disappeared. Through one coach after another they went trying to find him so that they could pay their fare. After they thought they must have been through every coach in the train at least twice, they looked around for a place to sit down until morning. Finding none, they opened a door with a little light over it marked "Men" and found themselves in a washroom. They cleaned some of the dirt and cow feed from their faces and hands. Charlie looked at us for approval as he added, "But we didn't wipe our dirty hands on any of those nice clean towels."

In the washroom was a big sofa on which the boys could have gone to sleep, but they didn't think it was

right to do that until they had found the conductor and
paid their fare. They heard a bell ring, and they were
starting down the aisle to find out where it was, when a
porter came out from behind one of the curtains. They
asked him where they could find the conductor, but he
laughed so hard he could hardly answer them. "Where
is he? He's up and down this train looking for two boys,
and you must be them." He put them in a compartment
and told them to stay there until he got the conductor.

When he brought the conductor back, Charlie handed
him the two new dollar bills right away, because he didn't
want him to think that they were trying to steal a ride.
The conductor looked puzzled, and when he asked,
"What's this for?" Charlie answered, "For two tickets.
We don't know the names of places, but we want to go
as far as that much money will take us."

The conductor sat down and ran his fingers through
his hair and looked as though he was "thinking hard."
He told the boys that he had been sure they were just
"spoofing" him about the fire, in order to get a chance to
sneak into the train. "And now," he said, "you're offering to pay your fare. I don't get it. I simply don't get
it." The boys asked excitedly if he meant that he hadn't
believed them and hadn't done anything about the fire.
They kept on talking until they convinced him that they
had been telling the truth and that he should do something "about the fire."

He got off at the next station and sent a telegram and
then came back and asked the boys for their names and
their home address. Charlie looked at the Court very
sheepishly as he said that they had given the conductor
their correct names and the address of the apartment
where they had formerly lived. We made no comment,

but Charlie assumed a defensive attitude as he explained that he thought that when someone asked for "your" home address that didn't mean the Home.

The faces of both of the boys lit up joyfully as Charlie told how the conductor had given them back their money, saying that the trip should be "on the company," since he was going to have to take them back to the city in case they would be needed to tell how the fire started.

When morning came, the conductor said he was going into the dining car to get his breakfast, and he would send the waiter for their order. The boys didn't quite understand what that meant, until a Negro in a stiff white coat came in and handed them a card, saying, "What'll you have?" When they saw the words, "Breakfast Menu" at the top of the card and under it a long list of things to eat, Tommy's eyes almost popped out of his head. "You mean we can have anything we want?" When the waiter said, "Yes," they scanned the list again and then said, "Bring us some of everything."

He did just that, and the boys' enjoyment of that food must have been something to witness. As Charlie described the different kinds of fruit they had, and the pancakes and sausages, and bacon and eggs, and all the other wonderful surprises under each of the big silver covers, Tommy's eyes danced with remembered pleasure.

The Court looked gratefully at the conductor as Charlie told about more of his kindness to them. He had not only answered all their questions but had also told them interesting things about many of the places they passed. He even took them up to the front of the train and had the engineer explain to them how the engine worked. They were truly sorry when they heard the porter come through the train, singing out, "Next stop will be New

Orleans." The trip had been so wonderful that they wanted it to last forever.

When the train stopped, the conductor told them to stay where they were until he came back for them. They saw him get off and then saw all the baggage being unloaded. When the last passenger and all the crew had left, the train gave a loud whistle and started into motion again. It chugged slowly across Canal Street and into the yards, and there it stopped again. The boys were back where they had started.

The engine pulled away, and the lights in the car went out, but the boys waited because they had promised the conductor. They were so glad when they heard him calling to them that they ran to meet him. Each of them took one of his hands and they laughingly told him that they thought he'd forgotten the number of their compartment.

If it hadn't been too dark for them to see the conductor's face, they might have guessed that he was half hoping that they hadn't waited. The two policemen who had been waiting at the station to pick up the boys were just a few steps behind the conductor.

Charlie wanted to say something more, but he looked at the conductor and his voice choked up. He hastily concluded his story with, "That's all we have to say. We thought he was our friend." The conductor was on his feet in a moment. "First of all," he said, "I want to put myself right with these boys. When I asked them to wait for me in the car, I didn't have the slightest idea that the police had been notified to pick them up. I had telephoned the Company's agent that I was bringing the boys in, just in case they would be needed to testify about the fire."

Then he turned on Smith. "These kids didn't rob you, and you know it. Your money was burned up in the pocket of that coat, where you put it after you counted it. I did testify that the boys had money when I found them on the train, but I remember now that it was just two new one-dollar bills, exactly as Charlie said. And they didn't assault you, either, unless you call it that when two boys try to get away from a guy who's kicking and abusing them and planning to turn them over to the sheriff to get out of paying them for four days' work."

His next remarks were addressed to the Court. He wanted to know if there wasn't something the law could do to a man for coaxing two kids into running away from home and then mistreating them.

Tommy interrupted him to say that "the man" wasn't to blame for their running away because they had already started to run away when he asked them to go with him. Then the conductor asked the Court belligerently why Tommy and Charlie had been put in an institution, "when anybody could see that all they needed was a good home." He was sure that the boys weren't "bad," and his eyes were moist with tears as he said, "They made me a promise, and they kept it because they thought I was their friend." He had to pause to regain possession of himself before he said, "You weren't mistaken, kids. I was your friend, and I'm still your friend, and I'm going to hire a lawyer to get you out of this trouble."

When he had finished, we asked him what he thought a lawyer could do for the boys. He answered, as we had expected, that maybe a lawyer could keep them from being put back in the Home from which they had run away, or in any other institution. We agreed with everything he had said about the boys' needing a home, but we told him that we were sure that he didn't realize how few good foster homes were available for children. We explained that foster parents were seldom willing to accept adolescent boys, especially in a case like this, where the Court was asking that the boys be placed together. The conductor was indignant at the very suggestion of separating Tommy and Charlie, and said it would be nothing short of a "crime."

The Probation Officer read the reports from all the public and private agencies, regretfully informing the Court that foster home placement for these boys was impossible. Then he read the request from the institution in which the boys had been placed, asking that they be relieved of custody. We asked the Probation Officer for his recommendation, and he threw up his hands in despair, saying, "I don't recommend it, but we have to put them some place, and the State Training School is the only place that can't turn us down."

The conductor's face was red with anger as he asked, "Do I understand that this Court is going to have to put these kids in a reform school, where you know they don't belong?" We answered his question with another. "What do you think we should do?"

We waited patiently for him to think it over. The solution of the problem had to come from him, without any suggestion from us. Tommy and Charlie looked at him, and all the faith that was in their hearts was reflected in their bright faces. He didn't fail them this time. The Court knew what he was going to say before he even started his long speech. But we let him do it his own way.

Before he had finished, he had given us a complete account of his whole life, a description of his wife and his home, and the names of numerous friends, neighbors, and employers who could vouch for his character. He told us exactly what his earnings were after taxes and deductions, and then he asked the boys if they would like to make their home with him if the Court would let them.

Charlie took Tommy by the hand and went over to him. The conductor was a big man, and as he stood there with a hand on the shoulder of each boy, he looked like a symbol of the protection which these boys so sorely needed.

An ominous silence fell upon all of us as the Probation Officer started to say something about investigation. But where were we going to put the boys in the meantime? When the officer thought about sending Tommy and Charlie to the Training School for even a short period, and about cases of which he knew in which generous offers had been withdrawn because of unavoidable delays in accepting them, he decided that this was one case in which he would prefer to "jeopardize" his standing as a careful Probation Officer, rather than jeopardize what he believed to be the one chance of saving these boys from delinquency.

You could have heard the proverbial pin drop as he announced his recommendations. "I recommend that Thomas and Charles Doe be placed in the custody of Mr. and Mrs. Thomas Waters, under the supervision of the Probation Department of the Court." The boys and the conductor were so excited and so busy thanking the Probation Officer that they could hardly have heard us say, "It is so ordered."

2

MOTHER LOVE

Each day in juvenile court is different from every other day. No two cases are alike. The problems of human beings are as complex and varied as life itself.

Yet, there are certain characteristics common to all people who seek help and guidance from the Court. They all feel they must tell their troubles to the judge. This is as true of those courts which are adequately staffed with social workers, psychiatrists, psychologists, and other experts as of those with very limited facilities.

In our court we began hearing cases at ten o'clock in the morning and went on without interruption until every matter on our docket had been disposed of. Because this usually left only a few hours in the late afternoon— all too short a time for the many people who felt that they needed to see us—we tried to crowd as many interviews as possible into the early morning hours.

Through some unforeseen circumstance, on the morning Daphne first came in to consult us, it happened that there was a short interval between the last interview and the hour for convening court. When Daphne refused to discuss the nature of her mission with anyone in the outer

office, the attendant showed her all the people who were
waiting for their cases to be called, so that she would understand that she could have only a few minutes with
the judge.

The door of our office looked nearby as the attendant
pointed it out to Daphne, but it seemed to her to be
farther and farther away as she walked up the aisle of
the crowded court room. She felt as though a thousand
eyes were fastened upon her, and she wanted to turn
around and run. It was her first experience in a court of
any kind, and it was unfortunate for her that our court,
like many others, was not designed for the purposes for
which it was being used. She looked around and saw
that there was no way to reach the office to which she
had been directed other than through the rows of bulg-
ing eyes which were so obviously fixed upon her. So she
forced herself to go on, trying to quicken her pace and to
look straight ahead but feeling every glance that was
turned in her direction.

When she appeared in our office, her face flushed with
embarrassment, she looked as though she wanted to cry.
Even so, we saw that she was a beautiful young woman.
The tears clouding her large blue eyes could not conceal
their depth and beauty; neither the quivering of her
sharply cleft chin nor the anxious frown wrinkling her
forehead could obscure the loveliness of a face like none
we had ever seen. She was well-groomed and exquisitely
dressed, but she would have been an appealing figure if
she had been wearing sack cloth.

As we looked at her we guessed that the people in the
outer courtroom may have been gazing at her in frank
admiration, which she had evidently misinterpreted as
rudeness. We tried to correct the impression by explain-

ing that most of those who were waiting outside had little to brighten their drab lives and that it was only natural that they should have noticed her. She was quick to respond to the implied compliment with a grateful smile, and she became more at ease.

She told us that no one knew that she was consulting us. She would have liked to confide in her husband, but that would have involved a disclosure which might have hurt him terribly. She looked very disturbed as she talked. "The trouble is that he thinks of me as one who could do no wrong. I wanted to tell him about my mistake before we were married, and I don't think that he would have minded so much then. But mother wouldn't hear of it. And it's too late now, because I'm afraid it would kill him if he found out that I've been deceiving him all these years."

This was an old story to us. Many wives and husbands are obsessed with feelings of guilt because of some youthful indiscretion they have concealed from their partners. But Daphne was blessed with a happy disposition, and she had been able to forget all about her mistake during the first years of her married life. She and her husband were very much in love, and Daphne said it looked as though she had everything that her heart could desire, until the doctors advised her that there was little possibility of her ever bearing a child. Then she suddenly knew that she wanted a child more than anything else in the world.

Her family doctor had suggested that she adopt a baby. Although her husband didn't take very kindly to the idea at first, he withdrew his objections and went with her to apply for a child. After going through the usual procedure, they were approved as prospective adoptive parents and were placed on a waiting list. In due course, they were advised that the agency had a child who was considered suitable for them. They rushed to the nursery in great haste. Daphne pronounced the baby "adorable," but after hesitating for a long time, she finally said she didn't think the child was the one for her. When the same thing happened with several other children, the agency asked Daphne to tell them frankly what she was seeking in a child. When Daphne said she didn't know, her name was temporarily removed from the list.

The agency worker liked Daphne and thought she had a great deal to offer a child, so the worker suggested that Daphne try to determine what was making it so difficult for her to decide. Not until then did Daphne begin to think of her own child and wonder what he would have been like.

She had waited many long, weary months for him to be born. Her parents had done everything possible to make things easy for her, but it had been necessary for her to leave home before she began to "show." Instead of touring Europe, as her friends and relatives supposed, she and her mother went to a distant state and lived there in seclusion for more than five months until her baby's birth. During all this time she never thought of her un-born child as anything other than a mortifying burden which was keeping her in exile for what seemed an interminable period. When her time came, she went down into the valley of the shadow of death and lingered there for many days. Even this did not make her realize that she had brought a human being into the world. Her mother told her that the child was a boy, but Daphne never asked to see him, nor did she inquire as to what was to become of him. She felt neither joy nor sorrow when she was told that the baby had died. It seemed no concern of hers. Her parents were handling everything.

Her recovery was rapid. She returned home to be received with open arms by her friends. Since she had emerged from her unfortunate experience with her reputation untouched by the slightest scandal, there seemed no reason why her life could not go on exactly as though nothing had ever happened.

There was still time to arrange for her "coming out" on her eighteenth birthday, which was what her parents had always planned. Through her father's wealth and influence and her mother's careful scheming, as well as by virtue of her own charm and beauty, she became the most feted debutante of the year. Leaders of society vied with each other for the privilege of entertaining in her honor, and she achieved the crowning glory of reigning as queen of one of the Mardi Gras balls.

After that there remained but one thing necessary for the complete and overwhelming success of her debut. She had to announce her engagement to one of the most eligible of the young men in the marriage market, and she had to do it before the end of the season. Daphne was well aware of all this, but she delayed her decision until the eleventh hour—and then she let her parents choose for her.

She hastened to assure us that she never had any reason to regret her parents' choice; in this as in all things they had known what was best for her. She and her husband were well-suited to each other. Both came from socially prominent families; neither had any interests outside the activities of the elite group to which they belonged. This was the life for which Daphne had been

educated. She never longed for anything more until she
became possessed of the desire for a child. The idea of
adoption appealed to her, and she was unable to understand why she couldn't accept any of the babies offered
her by the agency. Was it possible that she was rejecting
all these children because she was unconsciously seeking
a child who would resemble the one she had borne? She
asked herself this question and then realized that she had
never seen her own son.

Because neither her father nor her mother ever referred
to anything connected with her mistake, she knew they
hoped she had forgotten all about it. As a matter of fact,
she had thought of it very seldom until she began trying
to remember the baby she had never seen. She tortured
herself with futile attempts to picture him. Finally she
went to her mother and said that she had to know something about her child.

"What's the use of talking about something that's past
and done with?"

"But I can't even imagine what he was like. You know
I never saw him."

The last words were not intended to be a reproach.
Daphne was therefore shocked at the harshness of her
mother's voice as she replied, "He looked like a baby."

Tears of anger and disappointment filled Daphne's eyes
as she dashed out of the house without even saying "good-
bye." But the thought of her mother's never-failing love
and devotion made her go back to apologize for what she
had done. "I wasn't blaming you for anything, Mother.
I know you always did what was best."

"God knows I thought so at the time, but now I don't
know."

She burst into tears as she said this, and Daphne was alarmed at the vehemence of her grief. "Please don't cry, Mother. I promise I'll never mention it again."

"Talking about it won't do any good, but I'll tell you this much. He did look just like any other baby when he was born, but I saw him when he was three weeks old and he looked exactly like you."

She spoke as though each word was being wrung from her by some overpowering compulsion. Then she sank into a state of unconsciousness from which she never fully recovered.

The doctors who were called in shook their heads and said the prognosis was not good. After many weeks without their being able to revive her from the semicoma into which she had lapsed, they advised Daphne and her father that the end was near. The old family doctor stayed after the others had left. He took Daphne aside and spoke to her. "Try to make out what she's trying to say. I think there's something she wants to get off her mind before she goes."

Her mother's eyes were closed, and the pallor of death was already stealing over her face, but the dry parched lips were trying to form words which would not come. Daphne knelt beside the bed and listened intently, but all that she could hear was the sound of shallow, irregular breathing. Then she pressed her fresh, young face against her mother's cheek and kissed it. "Don't try to talk, Mother. Just go to sleep and when you wake up, everything will be all right."

But the dying woman seemed determined to use her last spark of strength in an effort to make herself understood. She opened her eyes and looked imploringly at her daughter as she tried to move the lips which refused to do her bidding. Suddenly Daphne knew what she was trying to say. "My baby didn't die. That's what you're trying to tell me, isn't it, Mother?" She nodded her head ever so slightly and then went to meet death with wide-open eyes filled with unspeakable pain and agony.

Daphne was overwhelmed with grief made all the more bitter by her conviction that she had been the cause of her mother's death.

But in the depths of her sorrow she could not avoid thinking of her child. The knowledge that he was still alive tormented her to the point of distraction. She didn't want to add to her father's worries, but she had to ask him to tell her what could be done to find out what had happened to her child. She knew that he was right when he said that she should not risk the loss of the good name which her mother had saved for her at such sacrifice. She saw that it would be unpardonable for her now to add ingratitude and disloyalty to all her other sins against her parents. Yet her heart cried out for the child whom she had thoughtlessly abandoned without so much as asking what was going to become of him.

This was why Daphne had come to us, and though she made no excuses for herself, it was obvious that she was sorely in need of sympathy and help. We first tried to have her understand that we didn't consider her entirely responsible for what had happened. Her mother had committed the first, and perhaps the most grievous, wrong by not letting her see her baby. Her lack of concern for the fate of a child she had never seen was no justification for the untruth her mother had told her about its death.

We had known a number of other cases in which fond parents had resorted to similar measures to protect erring daughters from the natural consequences of their own acts. We pitied the innocent, helpless babies who were the victims of this cruel injustice. We also felt sorry for the well-meaning parents, many of whom were destined to suffer remorse for the rest of their lives. But our hearts went out most of all to the young mothers thus deprived of the blessed privilege of holding their children in their arms before they parted with them forever.

We wanted to help Daphne in any way that we could, but we had to warn her that it might prove difficult, or even impossible, to locate her child. Her father knew no more than she did of the details of the baby's placement, for he too had supposed the child to be dead. In view of what we had learned from experience, as well as from what Daphne had told us about her mother, we doubted that the child's correct name had been revealed when it was placed. We remembered instances in which grandmothers had used their own maiden names in placing their daughters' illegitimate children, and we therefore suggested to Daphne that her mother might have done likewise. There was also the possibility that the baby might have been turned over to some individual under an entirely fictitious name, or under no name at all.

Although we had no reason to believe that the child had been brought back to our state, we checked the records of all our agencies and institutions. At our suggestion, Daphne went to the hospital in which the baby was born to obtain as much information as she could. She was disappointed to find that the hospital was under new management and that no one could tell her the whereabouts of any of the doctors or nurses who had attended her. We asked her if the baby's footprints were still on record, and when she reported that they were, we explained how important this might prove in identifying her child.

As there were no institutions or agencies for children in the town in which the hospital was located, our next task was to determine where the child had been taken or sent for placement. Daphne knew of several large cities which her mother sometimes visited. She went to each of these in turn, exhausting every possible source of information without being able to find a trace of her child. Then she traveled to more distant places to make inquiries and check records. When her efforts met with failure, she became sick and despondent.

Her husband had been very patient about these long absences from home; he hoped that a change of scenery would help her recover from the shock of her mother's death. But he didn't understand why Daphne always refused his offers to accompany her on these trips, and he thought that she looked more wan and haggard after she returned from each of them. When he began to fear that her health was becoming impaired, he asked her father to try to prevail upon her to remain at home and rest.

The daughter, who had always been so tractable and submissive, refused to listen to her father's advice. She told him that it would be impossible for her to know any peace until she learned the fate of her son, and she couldn't be persuaded to give up the search until her father agreed to take over full responsibility for trying to locate the child. He went about the matter with his usual businesslike efficiency, and Daphne was well-satisfied with the arrangements he made with lawyers and detectives who specialized in finding missing persons.

She resumed her plans for adopting a child, but she no longer referred to it as the baby she was going to adopt. She now talked about a little boy, and she converted the nursery into a playroom equipped with toys suitable for a growing child.

Her friends, persuading her that she had been in mourning long enough, induced her to rejoin the circles to which she had formerly contributed so much life and gaiety. She quickly regained her popularity, both as a guest and a hostess, and her husband rejoiced at what he regarded as her return to normalcy.

When her father noticed that she was inquiring less and less frequently about the progress being made by the investigators, he concluded that she was becoming resigned to the inevitable. He showed her a letter from one of the attorneys, containing a full account of all that had been done in the matter and suggesting that further investigation was not warranted. Daphne wouldn't agree to let her father discontinue the search. She told him that she was just an anxious as ever to find her boy and that if she appeared calm, it was only because the doctor had warned her that she might lose the child she was carrying if she didn't control her emotions.

Daphne's friends smiled knowingly at each other as they discussed the elaborate preparations she was making for the blessed event. "It's because it's her first," they said, "and it's been so long in coming." But Daphne knew this was not so. On the contrary, it was because her first child had come before she was ready for it and before she understood how dear it would be to her heart.

Both she and her husband assumed that the child would be a boy, but they were delighted when it turned out to be a beautiful little girl. She filled their lives so completely that they wondered how they had ever lived without her. As Daphne made plans for her little daughter, she couldn't help thinking how much they resembled the plans her mother had made for her. Like her mother, she was determined that nothing should spoil these plans.

Her happiness seemed to be so complete that her father didn't trouble to show her the perfunctory reports he was receiving from the investigators. It appeared to him that they had all but abandoned the case, and he was expecting them to end the matter of their own volition, when he received a wire saying that they had found the boy. In the earlier stages of the search, they had sometimes been very optimistic about clues which subsequently proved misleading, but they had never before made any such positive statement. Even so, he said nothing to Daphne before going to meet them.

He found them elated over their success and eager to tell him how they had found a clue and then lost it and then picked it up again. The child had been surrendered to an institution under a name somewhat similar to the maiden name of Daphne's mother. The records of the institution showed that he was not placed for adoption because it had been impossible to obtain any information about him. He was therefore transferred to another institution and remained there until he reached their age limit of two years. While in a third institution, efforts to clear him for adoption were renewed because he was a very attractive child who won the hearts of all who saw him. When it proved impossible to find out anything about his birth or history, he was transferred to a fourth institution, which was where the investigators had found him.

Each time he was transferred from one institution to another, his last name was spelled so differently as to be almost unrecognizable, and his first name was changed from David to Daniel, and then to Donald, and finally to Dalton.

Daphne's father was not impressed. Assuming that the child who was originally placed was Daphne's child, how did they know that this was the same child who was registered under four different names in as many institutions?

The investigators didn't know it until they had checked and eliminated every other child in each of the institutions. This left them with the six-year-old boy in the fourth institution, whose name was registered as Dalton but who insisted that he had always been called Danny. They had his footprints taken, and these checked with those of the child born to Daphne in the hospital.

When Daphne's father saw the child, he told the investigators that no identification would have been necessary. The boy's resemblance to his daughter was so striking that anyone who had ever seen her would know that this was her child. Closer examination revealed that the resemblance was not confined to coloring or other such superficial characteristics. There was not a line or a feature of the boy's face that was not a reproduction of Daphne's.

He had never thought of the child he was seeking as his grandson; but as the boy looked up at him and smilingly asked, "Who are you?" he wished with all his heart that he could have answered, "I'm your grandfather." What a joy it would be to take the little fellow home with him and give him all the things he had missed during the years he had lived in institutions! He had never had a son and had never longed for one, but he now felt that a man needed a grandson! Then he thought of Daphne's little girl and put a stop to all other thoughts. He placed his hand on the boy's head and said sadly, "I'm nobody that you know, son."

It wasn't easy for him to decide what he should do. He didn't want to deceive his daughter because he was deeply conscious of all the misery that had resulted from her mother's deception. Daphne's plans to adopt the boy would have to be abandoned, and it seemed cruel to let her find her child only to lose him again. It would be easier for her to give him up if she never saw him, and yet he felt that she should see him before she reached any decision. Was he half hoping that she would refuse to part with him, once she had seen him? Or did he believe that he owed this much to both the boy and his daughter? He asked himself these questions long after the answers had ceased to be of importance to anyone but himself.

Nothing that he said to Daphne suggested that there was any doubt in his mind as to the course she would have to follow.

"We've found your boy, daughter, but you won't be able to claim him."

"Are you sure he's mine, father?"

"I wish I wasn't so sure. But his resemblance to you is so startling that it almost took my breath away. You wouldn't fool anybody by going through the pretense of adopting him. You'll realize that when you see him."

The investigators arranged for Daphne to visit the child, without disclosing her identity. The matron assured them that if "the lady" they were sending was somebody who wanted to adopt Danny they should tell her that the boy could not be adopted. "It's no use for her to come here and fall in love with the boy like they all do, and then be disappointed when she finds out he can't be adopted." She was still doubtful when she was told that the purpose of the visit was a secret which the investigators were not at liberty to disclose. But she agreed to make the appointment, and she also made it a point to be on hand when "the lady" came.

She had a battery of questions all ready to fire at Daphne, but she was speechless with amazement when she saw her. Daphne was not as sensitive as she had been before she started her search for the child, but she was somewhat perturbed when the matron stared at her as though she were an apparition. "Perhaps there's been a mistake. I was supposed to have an appointment to see a little boy named Danny."

The matron drew her in and almost hugged her as she closed the door behind her. "There's no mistake, and there's no secret either. You're his mother and thank God you've come for him! He's been eating his heart out waiting for you!"

She was overjoyed, and she made no attempt to conceal it. She had grown very fond of Danny during the three years he had been in her care. And although he was already a year beyond the maximum age for the institution, she had opposed his being transferred to a home for older boys. She often said that she had seen many children come and go, but that Danny was different from all of them. "They all say they're waiting for their own mothers and fathers, but they'll go with anybody that will take them. But not Danny. It's his real mother he wants, and he's told the social workers and everybody else that he'll have no other. He dreams about her all the time and it would break your heart to hear him cry when he wakes up and finds she's gone."

The matron had little respect for parents who allowed their children to remain in institutions for years, but she had never tried to destroy Danny's faith in his mother. And now his faith was rewarded! His mother had come and she looked to be as sweet and good and beautiful as the lady of his dreams.

She was hurrying to tell the good news to her little charge when Daphne called to her, "Please don't tell him anything." The matron paused and looked at her doubtfully. Could it be that, in spite of all the boy's hopes and prayers, this woman was going to turn out to be like all the others? But it was impossible to believe such a thing of anyone who looked so much like the gentle and lovable Danny. The mother just wanted to surprise the boy! The matron smiled reassuringly at Daphne and then went for the boy and told him only that there was a visitor waiting to see him.

Danny was never very enthusiastic about visitors, even though they usually singled him out for special attention and favors. He hated being compelled to kiss strangers and sit on their laps, while they were asking him silly questions. But the matron noticed that on this particular occasion he seemed glad to obey her summons. She was sure he couldn't know who his visitor was, and, as a matter of fact, he didn't. But he hoped it was the nice man who had come to see him the previous week. The man hadn't brought him any gifts and he hadn't tried to kiss him, but Danny felt that he liked him. He was disappointed when he reached the door of the parlor and saw no one there but a lady. He stood irresolute for a few seconds and then walked slowly into the room.

Daphne's heart stood still as she saw the boy emerge from the shadows of the dark hallway. His little form

was erect, and his head was held high as he entered the
circle of light at the center of the room. He was a beautiful child, and his mother was moved to the very depths
of her being as she looked at him and knew that he was
indeed her son. In that moment of supreme happiness
she forgot all else save her pride and joy in beholding
her son for the first time. She extended her arms to him,
and he came to her without hesitation.

She pressed him to her heart and held him there, and
he responded to her caresses. But after a while he drew
back and looked at her intently. And then he was back
in her arms again, crying, "You're my mother." Daphne
tried to murmur, "Hush, child," but she gave up the attempt and let him call her "Mother" over and over again.
Each time he repeated the name, it seemed to take on
new tenderness and meaning. For he spoke the word as
though it were a term of endearment, expressing all the
love and faith which was in his heart.

His mother heard him and understood all that he was
trying to say. She embraced him again and knew another
brief moment of ecstasy as she felt his arms about her
neck and his head against her bosom. But she dared not
let herself drink too deeply of this cup of happiness. She
held him off at arm's length and tried to see him as he
would appear to others. She tilted his chin and looked
into his upturned face, and it was as though she were
gazing at her own image reflected in a mirror.

She remembered her father's words, and she recognized the futility of going through the procedure of adopting this child whose every feature was an exact tracing
of her own. She had known adoptive parents who seemed
pleased and flattered when their friends remarked that
the children looked like them. But Danny's resemblance

to her was too marked to be attributable to coincidence. It was incontrovertible evidence of the error of her youth.

Danny's eyes met hers as she was thinking of all this and his face was shining with faith and love as he said, "I always knew you would come for me."

The boy's trust and loyalty made what she had to do all the harder. How could she make him understand that other people's lives and happiness had become hopelessly involved with her own—that she could not bring disgrace upon herself without subjecting these others to the shame and retribution which she alone had earned? How explain to so young a child that she had brought him into the world under conditions which caused the law to brand him "illegitimate"? How could she expect him to believe that her sin, which had thus been visited upon him, would also be avenged upon her innocent little girl who was still an infant and whose whole life lay before her?

Danny saw that his mother was troubled by what he had said, and he hastened to assure her that he didn't mind waiting a little longer if she couldn't take him "right away." When she tearfully shook her head and tried to tell him that she was afraid she would never be able to have him, he reached up and patted her wet cheeks with both of his little hands. "It doesn't matter, Mother. It won't be so lonesome any more, because you'll come to see me sometimes, won't you?"

Daphne was sorely tempted by the thought his words suggested. She could let him go on living in this or some other institution, and she could pay for his board and expenses. This would help her feel that she was doing something for him, and he could go on loving her and believing in her. She could come to see him and bring him presents. How glad he would be to see her, and how the sight of him would ease the pain and longing in her own heart! He would always be hers, and he would never belong to anyone else. She could go on living her life in the rigorous, set social pattern which would assure the future happiness of her little daughter. She could eat her cake and have it too.

But could she? Could she be guilty of such deliberate cruelty towards the child who loved her so much?

He was nearly seven years old, and the social worker had told her that it would still be possible to place him for adoption if she made her decision immediately. A large part of his precious childhood had already been spent within the walls of institutions. Could she let her selfish desire to keep his love deprive him of a home for the rest of his life? Didn't she love him enough to sever the tie which in the end could mean only frustration and bitter disappointment for him?

She remembered that as a child she had wept over the stories of the birds who brought poison berries to their young rather than let them remain imprisoned in a cage. She had pitied the little creatures who opened their mouths wide and trustingly to receive the death potion which was thus fed to them. She had never thought of the mother bird who had been frantically searching for her little ones, only to find them shut in behind bars which made useless the wings God had given them. And never until now had she understood the depth and the strength of the love that made the mother destroy her fledglings rather than see them live without the sun and the treetops and all the other wonderful gifts of nature which were their birthright.

Daphne realized that she was the only one from whom her son would accept the bitter truth that his mother had given him up forever. Unless she liberated him, he was doomed to waste the golden years of his childhood in the bleak loneliness of institutional life. There was no way to release him without destroying his faith in her.

She began by trying to tell him why she couldn't adopt him. But she didn't get very far before he interrupted her. "But you don't have to adopt me. You're my own real mother." She asked him to listen to her, even if he didn't understand all that she was saying. "You may remember it when you are older, and then you'll know that your mother gave you up because it was the only thing she could do."

Danny burst into tears, as he asked incredulously, "You're not going to give me away, are you, Mother?" Daphne explained that she would have to surrender him to make him available for adoption. "There's a nice home waiting for you, Danny, but you can't go there unless I sign papers giving you over to your new mother and father."

"But I don't want to belong to anybody but you. I'll run away and they'll never be able to find me." He was trying to hold back the tears, but his mother could see that he was deeply hurt. She took him in her arms and begged him to try to understand that she didn't want to part with him but that she had to do it.

But Danny had no experience with grownups who didn't do exactly as they pleased. In his little world it was only the children who had to do things they didn't want to. He drew away from his mother's embrace, and his eyes were clouded with fear and doubt. Then a bell rang, loud and insistent, in the corridor of the building.

Years of obedience to the sound of that bell caused Danny to start up and move quickly towards the door. Then he rushed back into his mother's arms and sobbed as though his heart would break.

When the matron came in and asked him if he hadn't heard the bell, he clasped his little arms so tightly about his mother's neck that she could scarcely breathe. Daphne made a feeble attempt to loosen his grasp and then looked on helplessly as the matron exerted all her strength in her efforts to unclasp the boy's arms. When she saw that the big, powerful woman was annoyed at the child's resistance, she cried out in alarm, "Watch out, you might break his little arms."

The matron gave her a withering look which was even more expressive than the words which followed it. "I've been taking care of other people's children for more than thirty years, and I haven't broken any arms yet." She looked pityingly at Danny and glared angrily at his mother as she continued her tirade. "And I can tell you another thing, just in case you don't know it. A broken arm ain't near as hard to mend as a broken heart."

She pointed to the door and Danny looked hopefully at his mother to see if she would bid him stay. The matron sniffed contemptuously. She had no sympathy for the mothers of her wards, and she never ceased to wonder at the children's faith in them. She now thought that Danny's mother was like all the rest, and she had no intention of making things easier for her.

She let the boy stand there with his heart in his eyes, waiting for his mother to tell him that he no longer had to obey the rules of the institution. He waited in vain for a word, or a sign, or a gesture. Then he walked slowly from the room, with bent head and every vestige of hope and light gone from his face. His mother followed him to the door and watched the pitiful little figure as it proceeded down the long hallway. When he reached the end, he turned and raised one of his hands and managed a little smile for his mother as he waved good-bye to her forever.

Daphne gave the information necessary to make Danny available for adoption, and she executed a surrender in favor of an agency in the city in which she had found him. We were informed that he had been placed for adoption, but we had no way of learning the rest of his story. Daphne has told us that every time she sees a fine, upstanding young boy, she thinks of her son. She doesn't know that whenever we meet a maladjusted youth, whose aggressions against society have brought him into conflict with the law, we wonder if he was the victim of some refinement of cruelty inflicted in the name of mother love.

3

BAD GIRL

According to statistics of juvenile courts throughout the country, as well as those of the Federal Bureau of Investigation, a relatively small proportion of offenses involving violence can be attributed to youth of the female sex. Many theories have been advanced to explain this phenomenon, but most of them conflict with well-established facts.

For many decades, girls have been exposed to very much the same cultural norms and educational systems as have their brothers. Radio, television, comics, the movies, the press—all have an equal opportunity to influence the morals and behavior of children of both sexes. Poverty and unemployment, undesirable neighborhood conditions and lack of recreational facilities, poor housing and broken homes prevail to just about the same extent in the environment of one sex as the other. And certainly there is no reason to believe that children of the female sex are exempt from the frustrations, rejections, and other emotional disturbances and conflicts which are often considered responsible for aggressive behavior.

It has been suggested that sexual delinquency serves as an aggressive outlet for girls more frequently than it

does for boys, but even if we take this into account, the
ratio is still about five to one in favor of girls. It would
therefore appear that the explanation of the delinquency
differential between the sexes will have to be sought in
the differences in their temperaments and attitudes.

This is a subject which would seem to offer a fertile
field for research, but there are few juvenile courts in the
country equipped for anything like the penetrating and
intensive inquiry which such a study would require. Most
of us have to use such powers of insight and understanding as we possess, and the skill of such experts as are available to us, for the diagnosis and treatment of the particular individuals who come before us. While it is in-
disputable that courts have made some discoveries which
will ultimately lead to a better understanding of human
behavior, no program has as yet been instituted by which
their combined experiences may be added up and scien-
tifically examined and evaluated.

The differences between delinquents and non-delin-
quents are not as marked and measurable as was at one
time supposed, and it is sometimes impossible to predict
which children will resort to overt acts of violence if they
are subjected to pressures which overwhelm what are for
them the inhibiting considerations.

The general public has difficulty in understanding that
when this occurs there is no deterrent effective in pre-
venting the overt act. Nor is it easy for people to accept
the fact that maladjustments which produce these compelling situations are often too deep-rooted to respond to
belated diagnosis and treatment.

We have often asked ourselves the question, "How early
would we have had to detect and alter conditions in the
lives of children in order to have prevented the overt acts

for which they were brought before us?" In nearly every case, we concluded we would have had to intervene long before anyone but the parents had the opportunity to be aware of forces at work, developing traits and attitudes, which would subsequently combine with other factors to make the compulsion to commit the overt act irresistible.

This is true of girls as well as of boys. Experience shows that many of the children who yield to the impulse to commit an act of violence have never before shown any outward tendencies towards aggressive behavior. On the contrary, many of them appeared to have been extremely tractable and submissive. It was not until a number of factors combined at the same moment that a situation was produced in which they found the impulse to act so compelling that all other considerations became insignificant and unimportant.

It often appears that the same traits and factors could have existed, and the same circumstances arisen, without inducing an aggressive act, had it not been for some minor incident which seemed to tip the delicately balanced emotional reaction. But we always come back to the fundamental proposition that these children do not come to the attention of any authority outside their homes until it is too late to correct the conditions responsible for their emotional imbalance.

Almost any case that we could cite would illustrate this point, but the story of our "bad girl" is one which is impressive, because fear and repression had entered this child's life almost before she was born, without producing any outward symptoms of emotional maladjustment until a particular situation arose.

Her name was Winnie O'Niell, and she had been questioned by the police and the district attorney before she came to us. She had won the hearts of all the authorities, as well as the sympathies of the newspaper reporters and the general public. Even the severest critics of the juvenile court's reputed tendency to "coddle criminal children" conceded that this might be a case in which the "eye for an eye" penalty should not be demanded.

She looked sad and disconsolate when she first appeared before us. But two deep dimples appeared in her cheeks as she responded to our smile. For a full moment, she was a bright-eyed little girl, glad to be on friendly terms with us. Then her expression suddenly changed to one of deep despair. She drew away from us and looked at the floor intently, twisting her handkerchief into a tiny rope and fighting back the tears in her eyes, as she said, "You wouldn't like me, if you knew what I've done."

We glanced at the petition which was on our table and told her that we knew what she was supposed to have done, but that we would believe nothing until it had been proved. Most youngsters would have seized upon the latter part of our remark, but Winnie's reply showed that she was not concerned with the matter of proof. "You can believe it, because it's true. And what makes it worse, I'm not sorry I did it."

Before we could make any answer or comment, Winnie's mother appeared in the doorway. Her shabby black dress accentuated the pallor of her white skin and the frailty of her small form. She hesitated and looked about her uncertainly, and then her eyes met Winnie's and became suffused with a love and tenderness which transfigured her whole face. Neither mother nor child made any attempt to embrace or to indulge in any other outward demonstration of affection. But it was evident that there

was a bond between them which transcended the ordinary
tie between parent and child.

Winnie took her mother's hand and led her to our con-
ference table. She looked at us beseechingly as she said,
"This is Mama, please—" Her voice was so choked with
tears that she couldn't finish the sentence, but we knew
what she was trying to say. She had been too honest to
accept our proffered friendship for herself, but she was
asking us to be kind to her mother.

We would gladly have spared both of them the stigma
and the ordeal of a court appearance, but the transfer of
the case to our court represented a concession on the
part of the authorities, and the matter had to be adjudicated. We consoled ourselves with the thought that a
hearing in our private office would be far less painful than
the public trial in a criminal court with which Winnie
had at one time been threatened.

We asked Mrs. O'Niell to tell us something about her
family, and we learned from her that Winnie was the
eldest of three children. She was born ten years after
her parents' marriage and came as an unwelcome surprise
to her father, who had wanted no children.

Mr. O'Niell thought of children only as additional
mouths to feed. He was a hard-working man, but his
earnings were small and he was obsessed with a desire
to save the greater part of them. His only other interest
was in eating, but he would often let his enormous ap-
petite go unsatisfied rather than give his wife enough
money to buy food.

During the first years of their marriage his saving
habits had seemed like a virtue to his wife, whose previous acquaintance with men had been limited to three
hard-drinking, free-spending brothers. As compared with

them, her husband seemed "a good man," and she convinced herself that she should be willing to put up with
his bad temper in view of his freedom from bad habits.
Knowing how he felt about children, she had been thankful that God had not seen fit to send her any.

After more than nine years of marriage, when she did
become pregnant, she was afraid to tell her husband
about it. She put it off from day to day, waiting for the
opportune moment which never came. In the meantime,
she arranged to have a midwife confine her at home, so
that there would be no doctors or hospital bills. And it
was literally the eleventh hour before she was able to
bring herself to inform her husband of her condition; she
was already in the first stages of labor when she told him
that she was about to give birth to a child. If any hope
of sympathy or consideration lingered in her heart, it vanished quickly when he flew into a rage which made the
pains of childbirth seem as nothing by comparison.

Winnie was a healthy baby, and she gave very little
trouble, but her mother knelt down every night and
prayed that she wouldn't make her father angry by crying. The child learned to fear her father's displeasure
long before she learned to walk or talk.

The O'Niells' second child was born two years after
the first. The father was even more infuriated about her
arrival than he had been about the birth of Winnie. He
denounced his wife for deliberately burdening him with
a "house full of brats," and he raved and ranted about
having to support the family with no help from her. He
had always regarded his wife's inability to work outside
the home as a great hardship on him, and he now taunted
her with bitter accusations of laziness and stupidity. Mrs.
O'Niell, having long since discovered that she only added

fuel to the flame of his wrath by trying to defend herself, listened to him in silence and prayed that God would change his ways.

She called the new baby "Nancy" in the hope that the father might "take to her" if she bore his mother's name. She also delayed asking him for an increase in the food allowance, because she had once tried to assuage his anger by assuring him that four can eat as "cheap" as two. When all her efforts to placate him failed, and he continued to vent his ill temper upon her and upon the children, she began to wonder if she was right about his being a "good man." With all their faults, her brothers were kindhearted, and they never treated their wives and children as though they hated them. But if the thought of leaving her husband ever occurred to Mrs. O'Niell, she didn't entertain it for very long—she knew of no way in which she could provide her children with even the barest necessities of life.

When Winnie was six years old, and Nancy was four, their brother "Jamie" was born. The mother had become panic-stricken when she found that he was on the way. She hadn't finished paying the midwife for bringing the other children into the world, but she went to her in desperation and begged for help. When the midwife shook her head and said there was nothing that could be done, it was only the thought of Winnie and Nancy which kept Mrs. O'Niell from taking her own life.

Unlike his sisters, Jamie was a sickly baby from the very beginning. He suffered from colic and ear abscesses and many of the other painful ills which afflict infants. In spite of the mother's prayers, in which Winnie and Nancy now joined, he cried almost every night. Whether it was on this account, or for some other reason, the father seemed to resent Jamie more intensely than he did either of the girls. He cursed the mother for having borne such a puny, sickly child, and he finally ordered her to put the baby in the children's room and let him "holler his head off."

And so it came about that Winnie had to take over the responsibility of caring for Jamie at night. She did it gladly, for she loved her little brother with all her heart, and she often walked him all night long, when he was suffering so much that nothing else would quiet him. There were tears in the mother's eyes as she told of how gentle and patient Winnie had been with the sick baby. As the boy grew older, everything that he did seemed to irritate his father, and his mother and sisters tried to protect him by keeping him out of the father's way as much as possible.

The O'Niells lived in a "shot-gun" house, so called because the rooms were arranged one behind the other, and you could stand at the front door and shoot through to the back. Most people who lived in this type of dwelling used the room next to the kitchen as the dining room, but in the O'Niell home the room next to the parlor was used as the dining room and was separated from the kitchen by the two bedrooms. The father was the only member of the family who ate in the dining room, and in spite of the long distance his wife had to carry his meals, he demanded that they be served "piping hot." As far as the children were concerned, they considered it no hardship to have to eat in the kitchen, where they were somewhat removed from the full force of their father's angry cursing and swearing.

Mrs. O'Niell thought the neighbors must have a very low opinion of her, because her husband's voice could be

heard all the way to the end of the block as he hurled
at her the vilest of epithets. She said this was the reason she "stayed to herself" and was almost ashamed "to
bid anyone the time of the day." Winnie and Nancy
also imagined that the neighborhood children looked
down on them and were talking about them "behind their
backs." Jamie was the only one who didn't bother about
such things. He played on the sidewalk every evening
until he saw his father alight from the streetcar. Then
he left his playmates without a word and ran into the
house as fast as he could, yelling, "Papa's coming."

This was the signal for the mother to get the father's
dinner on the table and for the girls to take a last look
around the house and make sure that there was nothing
there that might bring on one of their father's dreadful
outbursts of rage. Then they helped Jamie get to bed so
that he wouldn't do anything to aggravate his father's ill
humor.

When Winnie was eight years old and Nancy was six,
the father decided that they should begin taking music
lessons. They had never been allowed to touch the big
piano, which had been part of the parlor furniture ever
since they could remember. They knew that it had belonged to their father's mother and that she had been a
musician, but they didn't dream that their father would
be willing to pay money for music lessons for them. As
a matter of fact, the lessons didn't cost him anything, because he arranged for Mrs. O'Niell to do some sewing for
the teacher in exchange for her services. She would
have been an indifferent teacher at best, but she didn't
even do her best for Winnie and Nancy; for she was far
more interested in the dresses the mother was making for

her than she was in the instruction of pupils who had neither talent nor aptitude for the piano.

The father never made any inquiry as to their progress, and the girls were beginning to think that he had forgotten that they were taking lessons, when he came home one evening and ordered them to play for him.

He always found fault with everything they did, and they fully expected him to burst into a fierce frenzy over their bad performance. Each of them played the single "piece" she had learned, and then they waited for the storm of their father's displeasure to descend upon them. They thought that they were "very lucky" indeed when his only comment was the gruff command, "Go on playing." He kept them at the piano for the rest of the evening, while he sat in his big easy chair and read the newspaper. And they were not permitted to stop playing until he was ready to go to bed, which was well past midnight.

This was the beginning of an ordeal which was repeated every night for the next four years. The girls had to be ready to start playing as soon as their father came home in the evening, and they didn't dare to stop until he decided to retire. This was never earlier than twelve o'clock, and on "really bad nights" they had to play until two or three o'clock the next morning. They were often so tired that they could hardly keep their fingers on the keys, and they came to hate the piano as much as they feared their father.

The mother wanted to intercede for them, but they begged her not to say anything, because they knew it would only make things worse. It was bad enough for them to have to keep on playing for long hours while their father was reading the paper, but it was much harder when he was "talking ugly" to their mother. No

matter how loud they played, they could hear him when
he was shouting and ranting at her, and they were always
afraid that he would carry out some of his terrible threats.

They had never seen their father strike their mother,
but he would often clench his fist and shake it in her face
and then pound it down on the table so hard that the
whole house would tremble. When this happened, they
were frightened out of their wits, but they had to try to
go on playing just as though they hadn't noticed anything.

The girls would have been even more afraid of their
father than they were if it hadn't been for their mother.
They knew she feared him too, and he was big and strong,
while she was small and weak. But they never doubted
her ability to protect them, if their father should attempt
to do them bodily harm. The mother always stayed up
with them, no matter how late he kept them playing, even
though it meant that she had to listen to his vile abuse
for hours on end. And she never failed to kneel down by
their bed to pray with them. To her children, this frail
woman seemed a tower of strength.

She had to get up very early every morning to cook
the father's breakfast, but she let the girls sleep as late
as possible to make up for the rest they missed at night.
And she didn't wake them at all on school holidays.

It was on one of these days that Jamie was waiting
impatiently for his sisters to get up, and yet trying not to
forget his mother's admonition to be quiet. There was
a "surprise" for breakfast, and he wanted to make his sisters guess what it was before they saw it. And so he
was listening intently for any sounds which would indi-
cate that they were awake. He was in the parlor looking out of the front door, when he thought he heard them
stirring. He turned quickly and made a dash for their

room without noticing that the cord from the big electric
lamp was in his path. Before he knew what had happened, his foot was caught and he and the lamp went
crashing to the floor together.

His mother and sisters heard the noise and ran to the
parlor. Jamie was more frightened than hurt, but the
large china lamp shade was "smashed to smithereens."
They picked up some of the pieces, and when it became
evident that it would be impossible to put them together,
they looked at each other in consternation and despair.
There was but one thought in all of their minds—what
will Papa say?

The mother knew what she had to do, and she did not
falter. She put on her threadbare coat, without stopping
to take off her house dress, and she reached into the locker
and brought out her old purse. She told the children she
was going to try to find a lamp shade similar to the one
which had been broken, and she tried to warn them that
it might take some time. "I'll go to the big store on Canal
Street first, but if they don't have it, I'll try all the others.
I may be gone for a while."

The girls knew she wouldn't "waste money" by riding
in the streetcar, but they were sure she would walk as
fast as she could. In spite of her parting words, they
began waiting for her return almost as soon as she had
left. The hot muffins, which were the "surprise," had
grown cold long before they thought of breakfast. They
pretended to eat a few bites to please Jamie, but Winnie
had such a lump in her throat that she couldn't swallow
a crumb, and Nancy had all she could do to keep Jamie
from seeing that she wanted to cry.

After they had cleared the table and washed the dishes,
they remembered that they had intended to help their

mother clean house that day. They went through the motions of sweeping and dusting, but they didn't do a very good job, because they couldn't keep their minds on what they were doing. They were watching the clock every minute and wondering how much longer it would be before their mother got back.

When twelve o'clock came, their hearts sank, for they knew their mother would be home by that time if she had succeeded in finding the lamp shade at the Canal Street store. She must have had to go farther. But how much farther? They kept asking themselves the question over and over.

They made some lunch for Jamie, but they were still too upset to eat anything, and they were also worried about their mother having to walk so far. They knew that she would keep going until she found the shade or until there were no more stores to try. Then they began to wonder if she would have enough money to buy the shade if she did finally find it. They had no idea as to what such an article would cost, and they knew that whatever it was, it would have to come out of "the eating money." Their father never allowed their mother to "charge" anything, and the only funds which ever came into her hands were the few dollars he gave her to buy food. But the girls felt that they would be willing to do without food forever to keep their father from getting angry about the broken shade.

Winnie and Nancy whispered to each other about what they were thinking, because they didn't want Jamie to know that they were losing hope. They told him to go outside and play after lunch, and when he didn't seem to want to go, Winnie said, "Let's pray." The three of them knelt down and begged God to let their mother find the shade.

They couldn't speak to God the way their mother did, but they repeated the same prayers hundreds of times, hoping that they might thus be able to make Him understand what was in their hearts. They had been on their knees for several hours when Jamie sank to the floor and fell asleep. The girls continued to kneel and pray.

It was nearly dark when their mother returned. She was dragging her feet, and her face looked worn and haggard. They knew without asking that she hadn't found the shade. She knelt down beside them, and Jamie woke up, and they all prayed together. The mother asked God to forgive them for anything they had done to offend Him. And when she ended with, "And please, dear God, don't let Papa be too angry," they burst into tears, because they didn't see how even God could manage that.

Then the mother hurried to the kitchen to cook dinner. She prepared dishes which the father particularly liked, hoping against hope that she might be able to put him in a "good humor." She wanted the girls to eat something, but they were afraid that the father would come in before they had finished. They washed their hands and set up their music on the piano, so that they could begin playing the moment he arrived. Nothing enraged him so much as any delay on their part in starting the "music."

He was late that night, for which they were thankful, and yet they were growing more anxious and fearful with every moment that passed. They almost wished that he'd come home and get it over with, only they didn't know what "it" would be and nothing was ever "over" with him. The mother was standing over the kitchen stove, stirring the pots. When the odor of her cooking reached the girls' nostrils, they suddenly realized that they were very hungry. It was nearly nine o'clock, and they had eaten nothing all day. But it was too late now. Their father was coming up the front steps.

By the time he opened the door, the girls were seated at the piano, playing a "duet." Their eyes were on the sheet of music which they were following, but they knew that he walked hastily through the parlor and sat down at the dining table without taking off his hat or coat. That meant that he was very hungry and would eat three or four helpings of everything. It would probably be an hour before he came back into the parlor and noticed that the lamp shade was missing. They breathed more easily and banged on the piano as loud as they could, because they knew that the louder the music, the better their father liked it.

But it wasn't loud enough to drown the sound of the angry roars which were soon reverberating through the house. Winnie motioned to Nancy to keep on playing, while she edged her way over to the dining room door. She peeped in and saw that her father's face was distorted by horrible grimaces, as he hurled his plate to the floor and lunged at the mother, cursing and threatening her for having served him food which was so hot that it had burned his mouth. Winnie watched with bated breath as she saw her poor, tired mother backing around the table in an effort to keep out of the range of that powerful arm. But the father was pursuing her relentlessly, and he would have overtaken her if Winnie had not pulled her into the parlor. This gave her a moment's respite, but the father soon followed her and would have been upon her if he hadn't stopped short. He had noticed the unusual brightness of the room, and he was

looking around for the source of the light. When he saw
that the other electric fixtures were unlit, his eyes traveled
around the room again. He suddenly realized what was
wrong. He pointed to the brightly burning lamp and
screamed, "Where's the shade?"

When he received no answer, he became so infuriated
that he could hardly speak. He sounded more like a wild
animal than a human being as he snarled, "Who broke
it? Where's Jamie?"

He knew very well that Jamie was in bed, and he was
starting in the direction of the children's room, when
Winnie said in a shaky voice, "I did it, Papa." He pushed
her aside and thundered at the top of his voice, "You're
lying. Jamie did it and I'll break his neck and every other
bone in his body." The mother was trembling with fear,
but she stepped in front of him and tried to divert his attention away from Jamie and back to herself by asking
him if his mouth was still hurting. He paused for a moment and was glaring at her with a savage expression,
when she fell in a limp heap at his feet.

Winnie tried in vain to lift her mother's inert form,
and then she cried out in desperation, "Mama, Mama,
please answer me, Mama, and tell me what to do." When
there was no response, she looked imploringly at her
father, but he made no move to help her. She had never
seen anyone die, but her mother seemed too cold and still
to be living. She called frantically to her sister, "Nancy,
come quick. I think Mama's dead."

Jamie had been in bed a long time, but he wasn't
asleep. He had put his head under the covers to try to
keep out the sound of his father's voice. When he heard
Winnie's cry, he jumped up and ran to the parlor. He
saw his mother lying on the floor, with the girls kneeling

beside her and crying pitifully. Without hesitation, he walked up to his father and said accusingly, "Just look what you've done."

The father was speechless with amazement. Never before had one of his children spoken thus to him. He knocked Jamie down with one swift blow and then kicked him as hard as he could. The boy was still screaming with pain, when the father seated himself at the dining table and called out, "Get me the rest of my dinner."

Winnie assumed that he was speaking to her, and she rose from her mother's side and walked towards the kitchen. As she was passing through her parents' room, she remembered that her father kept his pistol in the top drawer of the chest. She had always known it was there, for she had lain awake many nights listening for her father to get it and carry out his threat to kill her mother. But why should she think of it now? Her mother was dead and her father was waiting for his dinner, and she was on her way to the kitchen to get it for him. But she did think of it, and instead of passing the chest, she stopped in front of it, opened the drawer, and took out the pistol. She returned to the dining room holding the weapon out in front of her with both hands. When the father caught sight of her, he jumped up from the table and rushed toward her. Winnie stood perfectly still and pulled the trigger. The father seemed to fall at the first shot, but the pistol was an automatic and had fired several times before Winnie relaxed her finger. Then she dropped the automatic to the floor.

Nancy and Jamie ran to her, and she put an arm around each of them and led them back into the parlor. The three of them were kneeling alongside the mother when the police arrived.

The neighbors had heard the shots, but long acquaintance with Mr. O'Niell made them afraid to enter his
house without police protection. There was a difference
of opinion as to how many shots had been fired. The
closest neighbors thought they had heard five shots, but
some of the others counted only four. They all felt certain
that Mr. O'Niell had murdered his entire family, and they
expressed the hope that he had saved a shot for himself.

They crowded into the house when the police officers
and the ambulance came, and they were surprised to find
all the children alive and apparently unharmed. But Mrs.
O'Niell was still unconscious, and Mr. O'Niell was dead.

Winnie told them just what had happened, and not
one of the neighbors had a word of blame for her. But
the police officers were filled with righteous indignation.
"She admits her father never laid a hand on her, and yet
she ups and kills him. She's a bad girl, and it's murder
she'll be charged with if we have anything to do with it."

The internes applied restoratives to Mrs. O'Niell, and
when she regained consciousness, Winnie had to tell her
the story all over again. She listened without any display of emotion and then looked at Winnie sadly and said,
"Why didn't you leave it to God, Winnie? He would
have taken care of it in His own good time."

Winnie's explanation was very simple. "We had prayed
so hard for God to keep Papa from getting angry. But it
seemed like Papa was too much for God. And so when
I thought you were dead and I was the only one left to
protect Nancy and Jamie, I just asked Him to keep me
from being afraid. And He granted my prayer."

The District Attorney differed with the police officers
as to the charge which should be filed against Winnie.
The case therefore came to us, since we had jurisdiction

over a child her age when the offense was less than a
capital crime. It was not a case in which we had to weigh
the right of the general public to protection, against the
welfare of the individual child, for there was no reason
to believe that Winnie would ever again be impelled to
an outburst of aggression. But we were faced with the
difficult task of helping Winnie to overcome the emotional problems which would be the almost inevitable result of her experience.

We referred her to the guidance clinic for such help
as they could give her, and she understood that our own
counsel was available to her at all times. Her mother
cooperated with us to the fullest extent by moving to a
new neighborhood, sending the children to another school,
and doing everything else that we suggested.

But we were never able to dispel the dark shadow
which hangs over Winnie's life. She was not sorry for
what she had done, for she continued to feel that she
"had to do it," and yet she became increasingly morose
and unhappy. We can only hope that the healing hand
of time and the limitless mercy of her Heavenly Father
will eventually bring some measure of peace to her troubled heart and mind.

4

TARBRUSH

Recent publicity on the widespread use of narcotics by teen-agers has shocked the public into awareness of this serious threat to the welfare of the youth of our nation. Those presumed to have some knowledge of the subject are besieged with requests for an explanation of the problem. Many of the questions asked are based on incomplete statistics and are fraught with unwarranted implications, and too many of the answers take the form of dangerous generalizations.

Drug addiction is no exception to the rule that the problems of youth are interwoven with many other problems which are as complicated as life itself. It is just as impossible to point to a "typical" drug addict as to find an individual who typifies anything other than his own uniqueness.

In relating the story of Tarbrush, we do so without pretending that he represents any race or group, and without contending that his history justifies any positive conclusions as to the causal factors which inevitably lead to the use of narcotics. We have selected his case out of the many which we might have chosen, because his emo-

tional reactions impressed us as being comparatively easy
to discern and understand.

Tarbrush was a handsome boy, tall and well-built, with
sculptured features and skin as black and smooth as ebony.
He greeted us with an air of scornful indifference when
he was brought before us, but we suspected that he was
merely putting up a front to hide his fear and confusion.
It was his first time in court, and it was obvious that he
didn't know what to expect. Since we didn't know what
we could expect of him, we tried to feel our way by re-
sorting to a simple device that often tided us over the
difficult moment of our first meeting with a ward of the
Court. "What's your name, son?"

The question was not as patronizing as it might sound
to those who are not familiar with the customs of our part
of the country. It's just as natural for friendly whites in
the South to address young Negro boys as "son" as it is
for them to call very old Negroes "uncle." We had encountered few children of any age or race who did not
like to be asked their names. This was one question to
which they always knew the answer, no matter how disturbed and frightened they might be by the strange situation in which they found themselves.

But our question appeared to be the wrong one in this
case. The barriers which this boy was trying to erect
against us were not to be lowered so easily. He looked
at us defiantly, and his tone was extremely hostile as he
answered, "It don't matter what my name is. Everybody
calls me 'Tarbrush.'"

The bitterness in his voice warned us that we were
dealing with a resentment which must have stemmed
from many other factors besides the hated nickname.
Since it was part of our job to find out what those factors

were, we went on talking to him in the hope that he
would open a door through which we could not see
without his help.

"You're getting too big for nicknames. We see from
the record that your name is John. That's a good name,
and it's short too."

"Nobody would ever call me John. Tarbrush suits
me too well."

We could see that he wanted to stop talking and crawl
back into his shell. But we looked at him expectantly,
as though we were waiting for him to say something
more. The fact that he didn't want to disappoint us
confirmed our impression that he was not as callous as
he wished to appear. He was still a little on the defensive, though, and he tried not to let us see how deeply
he was affected by the matters of which he was speaking.

"I got that name when I was born. When my mother
saw me for the first time, she took one look at me and
said, 'He's as black as a tarbrush.' And the name's stuck
to me ever since. I'll never be able to get rid of it, and
it wouldn't do any good if I could, because I'd still be
as black as a tarbrush, no matter what they called me."

We understood how he felt when we learned that he
had grown up in a "mixed" neighborhood, in which light-
complexioned Negroes and poor whites lived in close
proximity and called each other "poor white trash" and
"niggers." There was some doubt as to which of these
elements stood lowest in the social scale, but the neighborhood children solved the problem by combining their
forces against Tarbrush. He was the only dark child in
the vicinity, and he furnished a target for the jeers of the
children of both races. Almost every time he came within range of their voices, they sang out to him, "Nigger,

nigger, never die, black face and shiny eye." Being out-
numbered by more than ten to one, there was nothing he
could do but run and hide his face.

His father and mother were light-skinned, as were also
his two sisters, Eloise and Ophelia, and his brother, Ben.
His mother's relatives looked so much like white people
that they could ride in the front part of the streetcars
whenever they wished. It was a long time before Tarbrush understood what his aunts and uncles and cousins
were talking about when they wondered where he had
come from. When they moved up North and he heard
talk about the fact that they were "passing," he didn't
understand what that meant either. Nor did he know
why his mother always looked very serious when his
father laughed hilariously and said, "They better watch
out that a little tarbrush don't come along and give them
away."

Nobody seemed willing to explain anything to him,
and it was not until he went to school that he realized
that his glossy black skin set him apart, not only from
white people, but from the people of his own race as
well. The school which he attended was for "colored
children" exclusively, and the principal and the teachers
were all light-complexioned members of the "colored
race." Tarbrush was always seated at the back of the
classroom, and he was seldom called upon to recite, although he raised his hand for every question. Nor was
he ever selected to lead the salute to the flag or to take
part in school plays and programs. The teachers seemed
to try to avoid looking at him, as though the very sight
of him hurt them and wounded their pride.

He was treated in very much the same way when he
went to the hospital. His father had been in favor of

taking him to the public hospital, where the operation he needed would be performed by white doctors, but his mother had insisted that "colored people should have confidence in their own doctors, if they expect them to amount to anything." She had her way about it, but she couldn't find the money for a private room, and so Tarbrush was put in a ward with nine other Negro boys. He was anything but invisible in the long, white room, with ivory beds and snowy linens, but the light-skinned doctors and nurses, who had a word and a smile for every other boy in the room, gave him only such attention as was absolutely necessary.

When Tarbrush was discharged from the hospital, the doctors advised his mother to keep him out of school until the following fall term. He was glad of this when he first heard about it, but he soon found time hanging heavily on his hands. His brother had been called into the service, and his sisters had gone to live in Chicago. Although all of them were much older than he, they were the nearest approach to companions that he had ever known. The house seemed so empty and lonely without them that he was tempted to ask his mother to let him visit his sisters. But he abandoned the idea when he remembered what his father had said about a tarbrush giving people away when they were trying to "pass."

He was wandering aimlessly along the banquette one day when the boy next door called out to him, "Hello, Tarbrush." He was a white child whose mother went to work every day and left him sitting in a chair at the window. Tarbrush had heard that he was a cripple, and he knew that his name was "Barney"; but because he thought that it would sound too familiar to say, "Hello Barney," he just answered, "Hello." Then he stood, first on one foot, and then on the other, and waited to see if the boy would say anything more. When Barney asked him how he felt, he went over to the window and told him he had had an operation. Barney said he knew it and would like to hear all about it, because he expected to study medicine and become a doctor some day. His pale face flushed with embarrassment as he asked timidly, "Do you think I could?"

Tarbrush had been more than pleased by Barney's friendly overtures, and he was flattered at being asked his opinion, but he had been hurt so many times that he was still on the defensive when he answered Barney's question. "I don't see why not. You're white, aren't you?"

Barney thought from this that Tarbrush didn't know about his affliction. He asked Tarbrush to come in so that he could show him "why not." Tarbrush felt too lonely to refuse the invitation, even though he knew his mother wouldn't approve of his going inside the white folks' house.

As he passed through several adjoining rooms before he reached the one in which Barney was seated, he noticed beautiful paintings and furnishings which he never would have expected in a house that didn't look very different from his own on the outside. But he knew instinctively that it wouldn't be good manners to remark upon anything he saw.

He had never dreamed that he could find it in his heart to be sorry for a white boy, but he was filled with a strange feeling of pity when Barney showed him his useless legs and told him that he might never again be able to walk. "You see what I mean, Tarbrush? How can I hope to be a doctor when I'm so badly crippled that I can't even go to school?"

Tarbrush was groping around in his mind for an answer that wouldn't hurt too much, when he suddenly thought it might help Barney to know that there were worse things than being crippled. It wasn't easy for him to talk about it, but he managed to blurt out, "That's not so bad. It's not like having a black skin."

Barney couldn't see that the color of one's skin mattered at all, and he tried to show Tarbrush that he was wrong in thinking that it did. Even though neither boy succeeded in convincing the other that he had nothing to worry about, both of them felt better for having talked frankly about the things that troubled them.

Then Tarbrush told Barney all that he could remember about his operation. The time flew by, and when Barney's mother came home from work she seemed pleased to find that Barney had company. She offered the boys some fruit and cakes, and when Tarbrush said he had to be going, she begged him to come back to see Barney the next day.

This was the beginning of a friendship which meant a great deal to both boys. They were very nearly the same age, and although Barney had spent less time in school, he was ahead of Tarbrush in some subjects. They helped each other until they were both on the same level, and then they went on together, reading and studying everything they could lay their hands on. When they had read and re-read all of Barney's books, Tarbrush went to the library to get others. The librarian was very nice about helping him select books, but she always told him not to get them dirty. Tarbrush felt sure that she was afraid that some of the black of his skin might rub off on the books. He was surprised to find that he was able to laugh when he told Barney about this, for there had been a time when he would have felt like crying.

Each of the boys seemed to find in the other the companion he had been needing. Barney's only confidant had been his mother, and he had felt obliged to conceal his worst fears about his future from her. But he told Tarbrush that he had overheard the doctors saying that if they couldn't arrest the disease which was eating away the bones of his legs, they might have to amputate. He was less worried about losing his legs than he was about being prevented from studying medicine and becoming a doctor. He was deeply touched when Tarbrush offered him the use of his strong, young body. "I'm big and husky, Barney. I could carry you around and it would be just like being a doctor myself."

When Tarbrush's mother discovered that he was spending all of his time at Barney's house, she said it would have to stop. Tarbrush tried to argue with her, but she found it hard to understand why her only dark-skinned child should want to associate with white people. "Listen to your mother, child. Nothing but trouble can come of black mixing with white." Tarbrush assured her that Barney and his mother were different from other white people and that they treated him as though he was just as good as they were. His mother was shocked at this, and she shook a warning finger at him as she remonstrated, "Hush, child, don't talk like that. Someone might hear you."

Someone did hear them, and it was Barney's mother. She had come to intercede for the boys, and she told Tarbrush to go over to her house while she talked with his mother. He wondered what she said, but he had to be satisfied with his mother's explanation. "It's not what she said. It's what she is. You can go there as much as you like." Tarbrush took his mother at her word, and thereafter he went home only to sleep. He knew more happiness in the days that followed than he had experienced in all the previous years of his life.

He had always considered himself very ugly, his only gauge of beauty having been the degree of lightness of complexion. Therefore he thought Barney's mother must be "joking" when she asked if she could paint his picture. He knew by this time that she had been an artist and that she had been forced to give up painting for the more lucrative employment which enabled her to support Barney and provide him with the medical attention he needed. But why should she want to paint him? Barney's skin was as white and transparent as alabaster, and there was something about his face that reminded Tarbrush of the saints whose pictures he had seen in the church. He was thinking of this when he replied to her with another question. "Why don't you paint Barney?"

She explained that she had tried many times, but that she had never been able to catch his expression. "It's not always easy to paint things the way you see them, Tarbrush. But if I could get you on canvas just as you look to me, I'd really have something."

Tarbrush posed for her every evening when she came home from work, as well as on Sundays and holidays. As the picture took form, he asked wonderingly, "Do I look like that to you?" She assured him that he did and that it was going to be the best thing she had ever done. After working on it for many months, she finally decided it was finished, and when she asked him if he would mind if she named it "Tarbrush," he told her that he was proud to have such a beautiful picture named for him. He didn't let her know that the title spoiled the picture for him.

She put it on exhibition at an art dealer's, and although she hated to part with it, she felt that she couldn't afford to refuse the handsome offer she received. Barney consoled her by saying that he'd buy it back some day if he ever got enough money.

When it was time for school to reopen for the fall term, Tarbrush took a high school entrance examination and passed it with flying colors. The boys in the new school were from all parts of the city, and a few of them were almost as dark as Tarbrush. But most of them were much older, and he overheard them talking about the fact that he looked like a "nigger" and talked like a white boy. He realized that constant association with Barney had caused him to lose the inflection considered characteristic of his race, but he couldn't do anything about it, any more than he could change the color of his skin. And the boys might never have accepted him if they hadn't discovered that his home work was always perfect and was available to them whenever they wanted to copy it.

He told Barney of everything that went on at school, and he imparted to him all the learning he acquired from his teachers. The two boys went over assignments and worked out problems together, just as though both of them were attending school.

When Tarbrush finally made friends with some of his classmates, Barney asked him to bring them to the house. They weren't anxious to visit a white boy, but they were too kind-hearted to refuse when they heard that Barney was a cripple, confined to his wheel chair.

They were a carefree and uninhibited group, who soon felt so much at home in Barney's house that they made it their regular meeting place and went there almost every day after school. Sometimes they played records or started crap games, and at other times they just sat around and talked. Nearly all of them were "chain smokers," and they occasionally brought in marihuana cigarettes. Tarbrush and Barney refused to try "the reefers" until they had looked up the word "marihuana" in a book and found that it was not "habit forming." Even then they wouldn't have smoked very many of the "sticks" if one of the boys hadn't devised a scheme for buying them "wholesale."

They pooled their funds and sought a reduced price from the peddler who operated in the neighborhood of the school. When he refused to "play ball," they trailed him until they saw him go up the back stairs behind an old building. They waited until he came down, and then they sneaked up the stairs and saw a dark man sitting in front of a table and pounding something that looked like dried leaves and flowers. They watched him as he pulverized the stuff and rolled it into cigarette papers. They knew they were in the right place.

Because they didn't think the man would be willing to deal with all of them, they crept downstairs to talk it over and decide who should handle the negotiations. When they said that the man would be more likely to trust Tarbrush than any of the rest of them, they were referring to the fact that he and the man were both very dark. Tarbrush knew this, but he also suspected that the others were afraid to go, and he wanted to show them that he wasn't. He took the money and went boldly up the stairs. When he reached the top, he stopped where the man could see him and waited to see what would happen. He coughed and shuffled his feet, but the man didn't even lift his head until Tarbrush went over to him and put money down on the table. Then he picked it up and after counting it very carefully, he handed Tarbrush sixteen cigarettes from the pile which he had made. This was twice as many as the money would have bought from the peddler and the boys were pleased with the bargain.

But even at "wholesale" prices, the marihuanas were expensive, and when the boys ran short of money, they started selling the cigarettes to their schoolmates. The profits which they made were enough to keep all of them supplied with "reefers," but after a while they didn't think they were getting much "kick" out of them. The dark man must have noticed that their business was falling off, because he asked Tarbrush if he needed any "caps." Tarbrush hardly knew what "caps" were, but he answered "yes" and listened to the man's directions when he told him to go to a room on the third floor of the next building and knock three times and then twice.

Some of the boys knew about "caps." They said they gave you a "real lift" and actually "carried you away." When the others heard this, they thought it would be fun to try them just once. They sold as many marihuanas as they could, and when they had accumulated fifty dollars, they turned the money over to Tarbrush and told him to get as much "stuff" as it would buy.

He had no reason to believe that this mission would be any more dangerous than his previous one, but he was trembling with fear as he felt his way up the three flights of dark stairs. Instead of knocking when he reached the room to which he had been directed, he turned around

and was about to go down again. Someone inside the
room must have heard him, because the door opened and
a voice called after him, "What do you want up here?"

The words were spoken in such a gruff tone that Tarbrush was afraid to say that he didn't want anything except to get away as fast as he could. Before he knew
it, the owner of the voice had him by the arm and
was repeating the question. Tarbrush managed to gasp,
"caps," and he was too frightened to resist when he felt
himself being pulled into the room. When the door had
been closed and a heavy bolt had been drawn, Tarbrush
surrendered the fifty dollars and received only a whispered promise that the "caps" would be delivered later.
He gave Barney's telephone number, but he doubted that
the boys would ever receive anything for the money
which they had given him.

When he went back to Barney's, he told the boys what
had happened, and they hovered around the telephone
all the afternoon. They were nearly ready to give up
when the call finally came, giving Tarbrush exactly ten
minutes to reach the place where the "caps" would be
delivered. He ran all the way and had hardly arrived
at the appointed spot when a car drove by him very
rapidly. Within a few minutes, the car had circled the
block and was driving past him again. It was close to
the curb the third time it came around, and it slowed up
as it neared him. He recognized the driver as the man
to whom he had given the money, and he saw him reach
out his hand and drop a small package in front of him.
The car was already out of sight by the time Tarbrush
had picked up the package.

The boys were waiting for him when he got back to
Barney's, but they decided that it was too late to try the

"caps" that evening. The next day, Saturday, gave them time to examine their purchase and decide what they were going to do with it. None of them knew very much about heroin, and they all had different ideas as to how it should be taken. They found a hypodermic syringe in the medicine cabinet and had dissolved one of the powders in a tall glass of water before they realized that they had diluted the "H" too much. They wasted another "cap" when the needle got clogged with undissolved particles. Someone finally suggested melting the powder in a small quantity of water and straining the solution through some cotton before it was put into the syringe. This looked as if it was going to work. Barney offered to take the first shot, because he knew how to find the vein in his arm. The doctors had often given him hypodermics, and he didn't even wince when the needle was plunged into his flesh. But it wasn't so easy to administer the drug to the other boys. They wanted to get what was coming to them, but they jerked away before they were even pricked, and the search for the vein had to start all over again. They finally tied tourniquets around each other's arms, and when they had all received their "jolts," Tarbrush said he thought he would skip his. When he saw that the others didn't take very kindly to this idea, he dissolved the last powder and buried the needle in his arm.

He remembered feeling very light and gay, and then he passed into a dreamy state. He wasn't asleep, because he knew where he was all the time, but Barney's living room seemed to be about a mile long and as high as the sky, and the voices of the boys sounded as though they were coming from a great distance. Soon there were others crowding around and praising everything that he did. He was still Tarbrush and he knew that his skin was still black, but it didn't matter any more, because he was the boy in the beautiful painting.

When Barney's mother came home, she thought the boys looked very tired, and she asked them what they had been doing. They answered "nothing," but they lingered long past their usual time and then went home and slept all night and most of the next day. When they compared notes, they found that none of them had suffered any ill effects, and they were glad they had tried it. One of the boys suggested doing it again, but all the others agreed with Barney when he said it was no use to start something you couldn't stop.

When school closed for the summer vacation, Tarbrush and Barney decided to study very hard so that Tarbrush could try to skip to the senior class. But they had hardly begun their ambitious project when Barney became very ill. His mother couldn't afford to stay home from work to take care of him, so Tarbrush never left his side. He followed the doctor's instructions meticulously and was never as much as a moment late in giving medicine or administering other treatment. He prepared meals and coaxed the sick boy to eat them and never seemed to tire of rubbing Barney's aching legs in an effort to relieve the pain. When all else failed, he tried to lull him to sleep by reading aloud for hour after hour.

The doctors declared that they had never witnessed such patience and efficiency in a nurse, but they didn't realize that everything that Tarbrush did was a labor of love. He would gladly have laid down his life if it could have helped Barney.

As the time for re-opening of school approached, Tarbrush decided to stay with Barney and take care of him until he was entirely well. But the doctors had other plans. They wanted to remove sections of the diseased bone from Barney's legs and graft new bone in its place. Before they could do this, it would be necessary to arrest the disease and this would require hospitalization for at least a year.

Barney's mother found that the money she had received for the picture, "Tarbrush," would be sufficient to pay the doctors and surgeons, but the prices charged for room and care at the private hospitals were entirely beyond her means. The public hospital was the only alternative. This meant that Tarbrush would be able to see Barney only once a week, on visiting days.

The whole course of life for Tarbrush was changed. He and Barney had been like brothers for three years, and he hardly had a thought of which Barney was not a part. He had often heard Barney's mother say that she didn't know what they would do without him, but he now found that he couldn't do without them. They didn't need him any more, and he no longer felt important to anyone.

His mother had gone back to work for her "white folks," because his father, who had "taken up" with a woman in the next block, contributed nothing to the support of the household. Her brother, Ben, was still in the service and seldom wrote. In one letter he had said that he thought Tarbrush was "smart" and that he might take him into business with him when he returned. But that might be a long time, and Tarbrush had to try to earn a few dollars so that he wouldn't have to ask his mother to buy his clothes and provide him with spending money.

He applied for a job selling papers, but the man said he hired only white boys. He added that he sometimes made exceptions for "light-complexioned colored boys," and this was all that was needed to send Tarbrush into the depths of despair.

When he learned that Ben was on his way home hope again welled up in his heart. He was the one member of the family who didn't act as though he was ashamed of Tarbrush, and it wouldn't be so lonesome around the house when he got back. He was a "big talker" and he'd have tall tales to tell about the foreign countries in which he had been stationed for the past two years.

When Ben arrived in New York, he telephoned to tell his folks that he had a surprise for them. He was bringing home a wife. It was even more of a surprise when they saw his wife. She was a young German girl, with blue eyes and blond hair and skin as white as a gardenia.

Both of Ben's sisters were home for the occasion, and his father was also there, standing beside his mother just as though nothing had happened between them. Ben introduced his wife to each of them as "Elsa," who smiled sweetly and said "Pleased to meet you" in perfect English. Then she saw Tarbrush, who was standing apart from the others and gazing in awestruck admiration at his brother's beautiful bride. She stared at him as though he were some inanimate object without human feelings or sensibilities. Turning to her husband, she asked, "And who is this?"

Ben put his arm around her and tried to lead her into the next room, but she pulled away from him and pointed to Tarbrush and spoke so slowly and distinctly that it was impossible not to hear and understand her words. "I mean the black one. Who is he?" A moment of death-like silence ensued before Ben's father touched him on the shoulder and said gently, "She has to know some time, son."

Ben cleared his throat and tried to say something, but he choked on the words and finally appealed to his father. "You tell her, Pop." Tarbrush saw him watching Elsa as though his life depended upon how she would be affected by what she was about to hear. The father made no attempt to soften the blow. "He's our youngest child, and he's Ben's brother. We call him Tarbrush."

Elsa recoiled as if her whole being revolted at the thought of what this meant to her. And then she began to cry very softly. The eyes of the whole family were fastened upon Ben and he knew what they were thinking. He was talking to them as well as to Elsa when he asked angrily, "What's it to you?"

But when he looked at his beautiful young wife and saw that she was crying, he no longer cared what his people thought about him. He took Elsa's hand in his and spoke to her as gently as though she were a little child who was afraid of the dark. "Listen to me, Honey. There's nothing for you to fret about. We'll go away somewhere, and you can forget everything you saw and heard today."

Elsa dried her eyes and withdrew her hand from Ben's as she whispered, "I can't ever forget it, not as long as I live." She picked up her bags and left the house without another word to anyone. Ben followed her but he returned the next day, alone and blind drunk. And from that time on, no one ever knew him to draw a sober breath.

Tarbrush was deeply wounded by what had happened, for he felt that the curse which was upon him was responsible for all the harm that had been done.

There seemed to be no place for him in his own family or anywhere else in the world. Night and day he brooded about it and became so despondent that he often wished he could die.

This was his state of mind when he was approached by two men whom he knew as Max and Tony. When they asked if he would like to make some "good money," his reply was as sharp as he could make it. "What d'you mean, good money? You fellows are dope pushers and there's nothing good about that kind of money."

But Max and Tony refused to take no for an answer. The drug business around Negro schools was getting to be a big thing, and they were missing out on it. They knew Tarbrush had dealt in marihuanas on a small scale, and they told him that those profits were "just peanuts" compared with what he could make by selling "H." They kept after him until he could no longer resist the temptation to try his luck at "making big money easy."

It didn't take him long to discover that Max and Tony hadn't exaggerated the possibilities of the dope racket. There seemed to be no limit to the demand for "the stuff," and they could get almost any price they asked for it. When they made him a full partner in the business, he quit school and told his mother that he had taken a job. Soon he was able to provide her with enough money to permit her to stop working out.

There was no reason why Tarbrush couldn't go home every night, but he usually preferred to stay in the old warehouse which served as the base from which he and his partners operated. It was also used as a "hang-out" by their customers, and it was one place in which neither race nor color made any difference. The youths who frequented this "junk joint" were concerned with little else besides finding the means of satisfying their craving for the drug. When they needed a "jolt," they would have gone to hell and faced the devil himself to get it.

The business was conducted on a strictly cash basis. Max said it didn't matter where the money came from. He knew that the "hypes" took valuable articles from their homes and sold them for just enough to buy one "powder." He also suspected that they stole from their friends and neighbors and even resorted to armed robbery at times in order to obtain the funds necessary to meet their ever-increasing need of "the stuff."

Tarbrush had ample opportunity to learn that it didn't take very many grains of heroin to "hook" a young person, and he also witnessed the torments endured by addicts when they were in the throes of "withdrawal sickness." They would lie around the warehouse, moaning and jerking, and unable to eat or sleep. Many of them would become nauseated and exhaust themselves with retching and vomiting, while others would suffer such excruciating pains and muscle cramps that they would cry like babies.

Tarbrush was too much engrossed in his own feelings to be very much affected by what was going on around him. He was "all keyed up" about Ben and Elsa and, most of all, about himself. He was aware that when the tension became unbearable he could find an avenue of escape in the drug which he peddled, for he had not forgotten the blissful hours of relaxation he had enjoyed on that memorable day when he and his schoolmates had tried "H-caps" just to see what they were like. He remembered what Barney had said about not playing around with something that might get the best of you, but he felt sure that he could take a "shot" now and then without getting a "burner." It was so easy for him to get as much "H" as he wanted that he found himself using it whenever he needed to get away from himself. Before he knew what was happening to him, he was "hooked."

He had been in the "racket" for less than six months when the "shutdowns" started. At first they were infrequent and of short duration. The word was "passed down the line" well in advance of a "crack-down," and the "pushers" had ample time to put in a supply to take care of their customers until it blew over. Things didn't really get tough until the federal agents moved in and pressured the police into making periodic raids. When this happened, the dealers would disappear for weeks at a time; upon reopening, they would send the price of "H" sky high to pay for protection. The peddlers passed the increase on to the users, who were thus made to bear the cost of protecting the suppliers from the laws which were enacted to protect the addicts.

When the raids became more frequent, and the "shutdowns" extended over longer and longer periods, Max thought of buying some heroin by the ounce and holding it until all the other peddlers were sold out. Then he could "stretch" it and sell it for many times what it had cost. Each of the partners put up five hundred dollars, and Max placed an order for three ounces of "pure" heroin, for which he paid fifteen hundred dollars, "cash in advance." The dealer said the big shots had laughed at him when he tried to buy "pure" heroin, but he assured Max that the "stuff" he got for him hadn't been cut more than once and that it could be cut again and "maybe twice again." This would give them at least twenty-five hundred grains which could be sold for at least a dollar a grain.

They had no way of testing the heroin, but according to an apothecary's scale which Max had bought, they were "shorted" on the weight by more than three hundred grains. Max said there was nothing they could do about it, and the three of them took the small package up to the attic of the warehouse and hid it behind the rafters. Nobody but the dealer knew they had it, and they made sure that no one saw where they put it.

It wasn't long before the dealers were closed again, and the peddlers were soon "cleaned out" of "H." Max waited until he thought the shortage was acute before he called Tony and Tarbrush and told them it was time to "move in for the kill."

They were in high spirits as they climbed to the top floor of the warehouse, with the scales, a supply of empty capsules, and sugar of milk. They had everything ready to begin the operation of "cutting" the heroin. Max reached into the hiding place for the "dope." He felt around for a few minutes and then turned on his partners and asked, "Did either of you move it?"

Tony pushed him out of the way. After groping behind the rafters for awhile, he said the package must have fallen down between the boards. He told Max to hold his feet and he went headfirst into the wall. When he came out he had nothing but a handful of dirty cobwebs.

The three of them almost tore the place apart, looking in every nook and crack and under every plank and board. After they had gone over every inch of the building, Max said, "It's no use to look any more. Somebody took it." He paused for a moment before he added, "Nobody but the three of us knew it was there."

Tony gave Tarbrush a dirty look and said, "It ain't hard to figure out who took it." He turned away quickly, but not before Max had caught his meaning. "Don't try to blame it on the nigger, Tony. That's too easy."

Tarbrush didn't know whether he was more angry at Tony for accusing him of stealing, or at Max for calling him a "nigger." He felt like killing both of them, but decided to go after Tony first, when he saw that he was trying to make a "getaway." He would have caught him if the ladder hadn't collapsed and pinned him to the floor below. Max managed to climb down from the attic and free Tarbrush, and then the two of them ran after Tony. They went up one alley and down the next but finally lost track of him and had to give up the chase.

When Max noticed that Tarbrush wasn't doing much talking, he asked him what was the matter. When he received no answer, he tried to explain that he had never suspected him of the theft. "I never thought you took it, Tarbrush. I knew it was Tony all the time." His tone was apologetic. Tarbrush decided that it was no use to be "sore" at him for having called him "nigger" to his face. He well knew that all white people called him that behind his back. "O.K.," he said.

He and Max looked for Tony in all his usual haunts. They didn't find him, but a few days later they learned that he had been arrested and charged with possession of two and a half ounces of heroin. Tarbrush was afraid he might inform on them, but Max was sure he wouldn't do that. "He's pretty low, but he's not that low."

Max made the rounds of all the dealers, and when he found all of them had gone away on a "long vacation," he told Tarbrush that they'd have to go out of business because they couldn't get anything to sell. Tarbrush said he was about fed up with the dope racket anyway, but he'd like to keep some of the "junk" for his own use. Then he learned that their reserve was entirely depleted, and he began to dread what was going to happen to him. The warehouse reeked with the stench of vomit and excretions from young addicts who had lost all sense of decency. He couldn't bear to think that he would soon be as badly off as any of them. He became so nervous and restless that he couldn't keep still for a second at a time, and when he began twitching and perspiring profusely, he knew he wasn't very far from the disgusting and painful stages of withdrawal.

He kept a close watch on all of the "hypes" who went in and out of the place, and when he saw one of them looking like he "had a new lease on life," he grabbed him and forced him to tell where he had bought the "H." The address was one of the new uptown housing projects, and it was hard to believe that a "pusher" would be operating in such a neighborhood. But Tarbrush was in such desperate straits that he was like a drowning man grasping at a straw. He hailed a taxi and went to the project on the off-chance that the boy had told him the truth. When he found one of the oldest "pushers" in the business holed up in one of the apartments, he ordered a month's supply of "caps." The peddler was demanding an exorbitant price, but Tarbrush offered him an additional bonus for immediate delivery. In spite of this incentive, the peddler broke two appointments and finally tried to call off the deal. He had become jittery because he had been tipped off that somebody was on their trail. It was best, he thought, to "lay low" for a while. When

Tarbrush persuaded him to make one last attempt to "connect," he resorted to all sorts of elaborate precautions to avoid detection.

But there must have been a leak somewhere, because a small boy came up to Tarbrush just a few minutes before he was to meet the peddler. The child couldn't have been more than five or six years old, and when Tarbrush refused to give him the five dollars he demanded for "information," he sang out, "You'll be sorry" and kept repeating it as though he were playing a game. He wouldn't stop until Tarbrush offered him a dollar to go away and let him alone. He accepted the money and ran off, but he looked over his shoulder and called back, "You better beat it."

Tarbrush wouldn't have heeded the warning even if it had come from a more reliable source. All considerations of possible danger paled into insignificance as compared with his pressing need for the drug. He continued to wait for the peddler, and he felt that his perseverance had been rewarded when the man arrived and gave him a tiny package with one hand and received the money from him in the other. But the exchange had hardly been made when two policemen appeared out of nowhere moving toward them. There was time for Tarbrush to drop the package before the officers reached them, but he held onto it and slipped it up his sleeve. The officers asked him for it, and when he refused to give it up, they searched him until they found it.

He didn't give them his correct age because he thought there was a much better chance of "beating the rap" in the criminal court than there was in the juvenile court. He had heard of cases where addicts and peddlers had been permitted to plead guilty to charges of "attempted" possession of narcotics in order to escape the minimum penalties fixed by statutes. He hoped that, with Max's help, he might be able to "get out of the jam" without letting his mother know anything about it, and he therefore gave the officers a fictitious name and address.

But he soon found that he had underestimated the zealousness of the police. They put him in a cell and refused to let him communicate with anyone. Then they offered to return some of his "caps" if he would inform on his "associates." He was suffering physical pain and mental anxiety which he knew could be relieved by the drug, but he had no intention of "squealing." He tried giving some "phoney" information, but when the police said they would have to check it, he admitted that he had made it up.

He spent a sleepless night, but he was still unwilling to talk the next morning. Then federal agents came in to question him, and they "tricked" him into revealing his age. And so, in spite of all that he had done to avoid our jurisdiction, his case was sent to our court.

We were much concerned about him because we knew we couldn't help him unless he cooperated with us and tried to help himself. And we also felt that he would need encouragement from his family and friends if he was to win out in the long, hard battle which we saw ahead of him.

He had refused to give our probation officer his correct name and address, and we thought he might persist in this attitude if we asked him for it directly. We talked to him for a while and then mentioned very casually that we were wondering how long it would be before his mother would begin worrying about him. He looked at the big calendar on the wall before he answered. "To-

day's Monday, and she's been expecting me to come home
and bring her money ever since Saturday."

"Do you think she'll report you to the police as missing?"

"Colored people never report anything to the police.
She won't know what to do. Maybe she'll ask Barney's
mother."

"And what will Barney's mother do?"

"She'll tell my mother not to worry. Then she'll start
worrying herself. I hope she don't tell Barney."

"You seem to think that Barney and his mother like
you a lot."

"I know they do. But I don't deserve it."

"They may be thinking that you've been badly hurt in
an accident, or even killed."

"That would be better than having them know what's
really happened."

"Are they the kind who would go back on you if they
found out you were in trouble?"

This last question goaded him into angry indignation.
"I'll let you see for yourself what kind of people they
are. You just get somebody to phone Barney's mother
and tell her about the mess I'm in."

Tarbrush never doubted for a moment that Barney's
mother would come to his rescue. But he could hardly
believe his eyes when he saw Barney being carried up
the stairs and into the hearing room. All thought of himself was forgotten as he looked reproachfully at Barney's
mother and cried out, "You shouldn't have let him come.
You know the doctors said he wasn't to be moved."

Barney's mother smiled indulgently at this outburst,
and her voice was low and sweet as she answered. "He
wanted to come, Tarbrush, and I was glad that he did.

He's taking a risk and he knows it, but we feel that nothing that could happen to him would be worse than not coming to you when you needed him."

Tarbrush turned to us to see if we had any conception of what this meant, and his face was shining with pride and joy, as he said simply, "These are my friends." They were indeed his friends, as we had good reason to know during the long, trying months which followed. They insisted upon having him examined by psychiatrists and other specialists recommended by Barney's doctors; and then after all the authorities agreed it would be necessary to send him to an institution, they did everything they could to help him understand that he was being committed for treatment rather than punishment. It was they who inspired him with hope and courage to keep up the fight against the drug habit until he had won it.

The doctors and the staff of the institution said he showed remarkable will power and determination, and they gave him much of the credit for the complete and permanent cure which they were able to effect. Tarbrush gave all the credit to Barney and his mother, for he felt that it was only through their unfailing faith in him that he had regained faith in himself.

5

HARRY'S CHILDREN

One of the gravest of all the problems confronting juvenile courts is the temporary detention of children while permanent plans are being made by their parents or relatives or by public and private agencies that handle placements for the courts. It is the consensus that detention should be avoided wherever possible, but the courts of large cities have found that it is impossible to eliminate detention entirely.

This is all the more regrettable in view of the fact that the facilities available for the detention of juveniles usually fall far short of what is considered ideal. A recent survey of the thousands of juvenile detention homes in this country revealed that very few meet what might be regarded as minimum standards. Most authorities agree that it is almost impossible to estimate how much resentment against society is built up in children while they are the inmates of detention homes which are neither equipped nor administered to meet their needs.

Everyone who has dealt with young people knows that they have a keen sense of justice and that they become reckless and embittered when they feel that they have been the victims of injustice. In addition, a period of time which might seem comparatively short to an adult seems like an eternity to a child who suddenly finds himself in strange surroundings under conditions that are often unintelligible to him.

The detention home used by our court was not under our administration or control, and although it was considered better than average in many respects, we tried not to let a child remain there any longer than was absolutely necessary. But even that was sometimes too long, as we shall see from the story of Randy and Bobbie.

These boys would never have been placed in detention at all if they had been apprehended during the day. But they were picked up at night, and they refused to give the police officers their names or their address. The officers guessed that they had run away from home and that their parents would soon be looking for them, but the juvenile court was closed, and the police were prohibited from taking children to precinct stations. They might have tried to get in touch with our probation officer, but they thought it was easier to take "kids" out to the detention home and let their parents find them there.

The boys had left home that morning intending nothing worse than playing hooky from school. Truancy was an offense of which they had often been unjustly accused; they hadn't dreamed that it could lead to their being arrested and placed in what was to them the equivalent of a jail.

Randy, the older of the two boys, was not yet thirteen, and Bobbie was just eleven. The sons of a minister, they had been motherless since a short time after Bobbie's birth. For the first few years after his wife's death, their father had tried to care for them without assistance other than that of an old nurse named Molly, who adored the minister and the children and revered the memory of their "dear departed mother."

Some people thought the boys were spoiled, but their father was satisfied with them until Frances, the church organist, began to point out their faults and the physical and moral dangers which were threatening them because of the absence of a mother's care. Even though he told her very frankly that he had never intended to remarry and that no one would ever be able to take the place his first wife held in his heart, she persisted in her efforts until she convinced him that the boys really needed a mother and that she was the only one who could fill the need.

Randy and Bobbie had always called their father "Daddy," but after Frances married him she wanted them to call him "Harry" and her "Frances." They gradually learned to do as she wished in this, as in other things, rather than incur the penalties of her displeasure. But they never learned to love her, and they turned more and more to Molly for sympathy and affection. They knew that whether they were right or wrong, they could always depend upon their old nurse to side with them.

Frances resented this, and Molly further antagonized her by singing the praises of her beautiful and beloved first mistress and by encouraging the boys to idolize their mother, whom they could hardly have remembered without her help. There was nothing that Frances could do about the boys' mother, but she could and did get rid of Molly.

This was a worse blow to the boys than their mother's death because it came at a time when they were fighting their stepmother's attempts to discipline them. Their father had let Frances assume full authority over them, and he had refused to interfere when she punished them by making them wash dishes and do other "sissie jobs" around the house. Nor did he protest when these tasks were assigned to them on a permanent basis after Frances found that Molly couldn't be replaced at anything less than double her salary.

As time went on, the boys unconsciously blamed Frances for their father's apparent indifference toward them. They thought she was deliberately trying to come between them and their father, and they believed that whenever he failed to take their part against her she was succeeding.

It didn't seem as though things could get any worse, but Frances "showed" them by presenting their father with twin daughters and pressing them into service as nurse maids. They appealed to Harry with all the earnestness at their command, begging him to rescue them from the taunts of the neighborhood children. "She makes us push that double perambulator around the block, and the other kids tease us and ask us if we have to wash the diapers too."

Harry reproved them for referring to their stepmother as "she," instead of calling her by name, but he promised to speak to her. Because the boys knew he was no match for Frances, they weren't surprised when they learned that she had outtalked him. They were even more disgusted when she won another victory over them by getting Harry to agree that they should no longer be permitted to come to the dinner table. After that they seldom saw their father except in church, where he seemed as far away from them as their dead mother.

When the twins were two years old, Frances gave birth to a third daughter, and she was filled with bitterness as she wondered why Harry's first wife had been able to give him two sons, while she could bring him nothing but girls. Determined to make it up to him in some other way, she decided to devote herself to the advancement of his career.

She well knew that Harry would have been happy to go on working forever among the poor people who made up his parish. But Frances was aware that, even in the ministry, success is measured by the size of a church and the wealth of parishioners, rather than the good that is accomplished. It was largely through her work and her efforts that Harry received the offer of a "rich" church.

Much persuasion was needed to induce Harry to consider the offer, but Frances insisted that it would be very selfish of him to forego all the advantages to his children that would go along with the new ministry. She suggested that they might be able to hire a competent maid with the increased salary he would receive, and she described the extensive grounds of the new rectory. Although she didn't particularly mention the boys in connection with these advantages, she knew that Harry was thinking of them when he decided to accept the new assignment.

They hadn't been in the new rectory very long when it became evident that Frances had no intention of letting the boys "ruin" the beautiful lawns by playing on them. The only time they were permitted to walk on the grass was when they were mowing it, and weeding the flower gardens was added to their other hateful chores. The new maid was kept so busy preparing for the afternoon teas and other entertainments which Frances considered essential to Harry's new position that she had no time to relieve the boys of any of their household duties.

Randy and Bobbie still had to look after the babies, and sometimes they had to bring them into the parlor to be admired by their stepmother's guests. Some of the visitors noticed that the boys looked rather awkward and miserable on these occasions, and it was in a spirit of kindness that they asked who they were. Frances invariably answered, "Oh, those are Harry's children," and she didn't always wait until they had left the room before she began telling of all the trouble they had given her.

The boys retaliated by referring to their little sisters as "Frances' children" and by describing them as "little devils" whenever they had the opportunity. Frances told their father about this, and he couldn't understand why the little girls would squeal with delight at the very sight of the brothers who were so "mean" to them.

Randy had been attending school for two years and Bobbie had just finished his first year when Frances married their father. Until then they had been well-liked by their teachers, but there was a gradual change in their attitude toward school after their stepmother came into their home. They were frequently tardy, and they were absent so often that it became difficult for them to keep up with their classes. After the babies came, Frances kept them home for weeks at a time, and she was too busy to write excuses for them when she sent them back.

When they were questioned about their unexcused absences, they answered evasively rather than admit that they had been kept home to "mind babies." This usually resulted in their being sent to the principal's office, where they had to listen to long lectures about how shameful it was for a minister's son to play hooky. They were warned over and over again and were told that it was only because their father was a "man of God" that they hadn't been referred to the attendance department.

But they continued to let their teachers believe that they were truanting until the school authorities threatened to take the matter up with their father. They didn't want to disgrace Harry, and so they made a full disclosure of the facts responsible for their absences. They knew they were telling the truth, and they were amazed when the principal and the teachers said they didn't believe them.

The truant officer was dispatched to their home, and Frances pretended to be surprised when he showed her the boys' attendance records. She told him in strict confidence that Randy and Bobbie had always been behavior problems and that she had married their father in the hope of being able to do something with them; but they had proved incorrigible, and she was sure they were going to be juvenile delinquents.

The officer reported all this to the school, and even though the boys attended more regularly, they became the object of their teachers' distrust and suspicion. Whenever anything went wrong, they were called for questioning. When the proceeds of a collection for the charity chest disappeared from the principal's office, Randy and Bobbie were mortified to find that they were suspected of having stolen money intended for the poor. The bitter thought that they were considered capable of such a despicable act rankled in their hearts long after it was discovered that the money had been called for by a representative of the chest during the principal's absence from her office.

As the boys became convinced that everyone was against them, they sought refuge in an attitude of reckless indifference. Having heard so much about the evils of truancy, it was probably natural that they should think of it at a time when they wanted to show themselves and everyone else that they didn't care about anything. They set out one fine morning bent upon playing hooky, not because they wanted to go anywhere in particular, but because it was the only bad thing they could think of doing.

The sun was shining brightly when they turned their steps in the opposite direction from their school, but they had been walking less than an hour when they were caught in a cloudburst. They hadn't thought to bring their jackets, and they were wondering where they could seek shelter from the beating rain when a streetcar stopped directly in front of them to discharge a passenger. They climbed into the car, and after they had paid their fare, they had only six cents left from their lunch money.

The rain was still coming down in torrents when they reached the business section. The boys knew they would owe another fare if they remained in the car after the conductor reversed the trolley for the return trip. They were starting toward the rear exit when a crowd of passengers surged in with dripping umbrellas and wet raincoats and made it easier for them to stay in the car than to get out. They rode all the way to the end of the line without paying, but not without some qualms of conscience. It was the first "dishonest" act they had ever committed, and they were ashamed to look at the conductor when they passed him on their way out.

The car line ended in a sparsely settled suburb entirely unfamiliar to the boys. They walked along aimlessly—without any idea of where the street on which they were traveling would lead them. The rain had become a light drizzle that looked like a shimmering, transparent curtain when the rays of the sun began to shine through. The boys thought it was "pretty enough to be a picture," but they were even more delighted with the rainbow they saw forming in the sky.

"That's good luck, isn't it, Randy?"

"It must be. I know Molly always said a rainbow was a lucky sign."

"It looks like it's working for us already. I believe we're getting to the country."

They quickened their pace in eager anticipation of all the wonders they would see in the wide, open spaces ahead of them. Though they encountered none of the big ranches with roughriding cowboys rounding up herds of cattle which they associated with the country, they found that the vast cutover land was teeming with friendly creatures of every kind.

The grasshoppers "spit tobacco" for them in a most obliging manner, and any number of locusts and crickets were willing to stay in their pockets and sing lustily whenever their backs were scratched. They came upon many cottontail rabbits sitting upright on pine stumps, looking for all the world like Easter bunnies. Even the squirrels stopped to look at the boys long enough to show that they weren't afraid.

Randy climbed a tree to restore two tiny sparrows to the nest from which they had fallen, and a covey of quail startled both boys into laughter by rising suddenly and noisily from the ground.

They could hardly take a step without seeing something that was interesting. But the most exciting event of the day occurred when a half-starved dog came up and acted as though he wanted to make friends with them. He cringed and whined a little, as though he were afraid of being repulsed, but he capered with joy when he saw how the boys welcomed his overtures.

The poor mongrel had never known such attention as the two boys now lavished upon him. They had never been permitted to have a dog of their own, or even to play with dogs belonging to other children. After they had petted and hugged him to their hearts' content, they decided to call him "Pal," and he lived up to his name by trotting along beside them as though he had always belonged to them.

When they stopped to rest, Pal lay down and rested too. He was up again in a few minutes, coaxing the boys to romp and play with him. It was lots of fun to play hide and seek with him, and to see him do their bidding when they threw sticks for him to fetch. He also did his best to cooperate when they tried to teach him some tricks, but it was time to start for home before he finally learned his "lessons."

"We'll teach you some more next time, but we've got to go now, Pal. You stay right here and don't you dare get lost before we come back."

Pal wagged his tail and looked up at them with his soft brown eyes as though he understood every word of what they were saying. But he refused to be left behind.

The boys knew they couldn't take him home. When they saw that he was continuing to follow them, they tried to hide. Pal made a pretense of not being able to find them and then yelped with joy as he pounced upon them in their hiding place. He quieted down when the boys explained that they weren't playing games any more, but he tagged along at their heels, being still with them when they reached the suburb from which they had started.

Expecting to find their way back to the city by following the car line, they must have walked many miles looking for the street with the tracks. When it began to grow dark, they went into a small shop to ask for directions.

The storekeeper looked at them so suspiciously that they decided to make a purchase before asking for information. "Please, sir, we want to buy some food for our dog. We've got six cents." The man took the money as he handed them two bread rolls and pushed them out the door before they had mustered enough courage to ask him how they could find the car tracks.

Pal was waiting outside. They gave him the rolls and watched him devour them to the last crumb. Then they walked up one street and down another, but when they found themselves back at the store, they gave up all hope of finding their way home that night. They knew then that they had been going in circles, and they decided to sit down on the steps of the shop and wait for morning. It wasn't long before both boys had fallen asleep. The next thing they remembered was a blinding light flashed in their faces. They looked up quickly and saw two men in a car, which went by very slowly, then backed up and stopped in front of the store. One of the men got out of the car and came toward them, holding a flashlight in one hand and a revolver in the other. Pal gave a low growl and plunged toward the man with incredible swiftness. A shot rang out and Pal fell over. He lifted his head and tried to get up, and then he dropped back into a pool of blood.

The revolver was pointing directly at Randy and Bobbie as they ran to Pal. By then the second man was out of the car; he held up his hand and cried out to his companion, "Hold it, Sergeant, they're just kids." The sergeant shoved his revolver into the holster under his coat and came over to them. "I'm sorry about the dog, but I couldn't afford to take any chances." Then he pointed to a shiny badge under his lapel. "He should have known better than try to attack a police officer."

Bobbie, who had been bending over the lifeless body of the dog, straightened up at this, his eyes filled with tears, and said reproachfully, "You had no right to kill him, even if you are a policeman."

The officers looked at each other. Neither of them knew how to answer Bobbie when he added piteously, "He was the only friend we had, and he wanted to protect us when he saw you pointing that pistol at us. That wasn't bad, was it, Mister?"

The boys knelt down beside Pal, and Randy felt his heart to see if it had stopped beating. It was hard to believe that all life had gone out of him so quickly. Bobbie lifted one of the limp paws and stroked it lovingly as he blurted out, "We were teaching him to give you his paw, and he had almost learnt."

The officers were not so old that they couldn't remember what a dog can mean to a boy, but they tried to hide their feelings by questioning Randy and Bobbie sharply. When the boys responded in like manner and refused to give their names or their address, the officers felt justified in hustling them into the police car and driving them out to the detention home.

It was after nine when they brought the boys into the office of the home and turned them over to an old man who looked half-asleep. The officers became impatient when he began to fumble around the desk as though he didn't know what he was looking for. "Make it snappy, grandpa. We can't wait all night."

"Why do you always have to bring kids in here at night? Can't you ever catch one in the daytime?"

"That'll be enough out of you. Just give us a receipt for two kids, names unknown, and we'll let it go at that."

They were handed a slip of paper by the old man, who continued grumbling to himself long after they had departed. The boys wanted to ask what was going to happen to them, but the old man put his head down on the desk and continued to mumble until he fell asleep and began to snore. Although he woke up with a start when the telephone rang, he took his time about answering it. "Hello! Yes, that's right. I've got two kids here. They wouldn't give their names, but they might be the ones you're looking for. No, I don't know anything about descriptions. You'll have to come out here and see for yourself, but you'd better hurry up because if you don't get here before it's time for me to knock off, I'll have to take them up to temporary detention."

He went back to his desk without a word to the boys, but they felt sure that it was Harry who had telephoned and that he'd come for them. They hoped he would come alone, because they wanted to tell him that they were sorry for having played hooky and they would never do anything like that again. They knew he would believe them if Frances weren't there to spoil everything.

Knowing that their father was coming for them made the boys bold enough to ask the old man if they could sit down on the long bench at one side of the office. He grunted indifferently and then looked at the clock and began complaining about the lateness of the hour. "People ought to start looking for their children before this time of night. If I was a judge, I'd put the parents in jail when the kids step out of line. That'd teach 'em."

It was eleven o'clock when Harry arrived, and, although Frances was with him, she didn't act like herself at first. She stayed near the door and kept so quiet that the boys forgot she was there while they had a heart-to-heart talk with their father. They cried a little as they described Pal and the way he met his death at the hands of the policeman. They impressed their father as being truly penitent for all the "bad things" they had done. Knowing that their relationship with their stepmother troubled their father more than anything else, they promised to try "real hard" to get along better with her.

Harry was deeply touched by their repentant attitude. He looked at Frances to see if she understood the full import of what they were saying. The boys' eyes followed their father's. They saw that their stepmother's face looked uglier than they had ever seen it.

"Did you hear that, Frances? The boys aren't going to give you any more trouble after this!"

"They're not going to give me any more trouble because I'm not going to let them. If you bring them home, I'll leave you, and I'll never come back again!"

Vainly Harry tried to argue with her and get her to listen to reason. The boys had provided her with a plausible excuse for making their father choose between them and her, and she was determined to put him to the test. Her knowledge of the many considerations which would enter into the minister's decision did not prevent her from

believing that his abandonment of his sons would be
proof of his greater love for her.

She continued to press this ultimatum upon him until
the old man closed his desk with a bang and said testily,
"Make up your minds one way or the other. I've got to
start upstairs with these kids if you're not going to take
them home."

Harry held his head in his hands, groaning as he rocked
it back and forth. Frances accepted this as his answer,
grimly conscious that he would experience no such agony
in parting from her. Her victory lost some of its sweet-
ness by the bitterness of his grief. But she had the satisfaction of seeing the tragic expression on the boys' faces
as she placed a hand on Harry's heaving shoulders and
said, "I knew you'd see it my way."

The old man rattled his keys impatiently. "What's the
verdict? Do they go or do they stay?" The boys heard
Frances say, "Take them upstairs." Their father remained
silent, making no move to countermand the order. His
face was still buried in his hands as his boys were taken
away.

They followed the old man up the stairs. When they
reached the top of the fourth flight, he unlocked a big
iron door and pushed them into a brightly lighted room.
He was wheezing and gasping for breath, but he managed to tell the boys to take off all their clothes except
their underwear. As soon as they had done so he tucked
their clothes under his arm and went off.

The heavy door slammed shut, and the boys found
themselves in a long dormitory with rows of double-
decker bunks extending from one end to the other. The
occupants of the upper bunks stirred uneasily and drew
their arms over their eyes as though trying to shut out

the brilliant lights shining in their faces, but no one spoke to the bewildered boys who were waiting for someone to tell them what to do next.

They were heartsick and frightened as they looked around the room, realizing that they were imprisoned in a place different from anything they had ever known. Were they supposed to go to bed in their underwear? They had never done such a thing, but they found an empty bunk and climbed into it.

A loud bell which sounded like a fire alarm awakened them the next morning. When they peered out of their bunk, they saw a bespectacled young man standing at one end of the room, calling out names and handing out clothing. They didn't hear their names called, but they jumped up and asked for their clothes. The young man hardly glanced at them. "You're not going anywhere," he said curtly. Then he went out, taking with him the boys to whom he had given clothing and letting Randy and Bobbie find out for themselves that underwear was the uniform of the temporary detention dormitory.

They also learned that the boys who had left were referred to as "transients" by the eight husky fellows remaining in the dormitory who called themselves "regulars." They appeared to be a "pretty tough bunch," loud-mouthed and profane. They may have been showing off for the benefit of the newcomers; none had a word to say to the young man when he brought in two big cans and a box of bread and told them to eat their breakfast.

The door had hardly closed on him before the big boys were cursing and swearing about the food he had brought. They reserved their worst epithets for the can marked "cereal." They said it tasted like poison because it had been cooked without salt. The other can contained strong

black coffee, which they all drank, though it was difficult to drink from the tin plates which served as cups.
It was terrifying to hear the howls of rage as the smok-
ing, hot liquid spilled out of the plates and over their
bodies on the way to their lips. Some persevered until
they managed to gulp a few mouthfuls; others gave up
in disgust and threw their plates to the far corner of the
room.

After the last of the big boys had finished eating and
had lounged off in the direction of the bathroom, Randy
and Bobbie crept over to the food. They skipped the
cereal after what they had heard about it, and they didn't
think black coffee without sugar or cream was worth all
the trouble of trying to balance it on a plate. But there
was plenty of bread and no one to stop them from eating
their fill.

The big boys emerged from the bathroom, dripping
wet and denouncing the home and everyone connected
with it for not providing towels. Some of them blamed
the young man with the spectacles for always being in
too much of a hurry to find out what they needed. "He
barges in and rushes out like he's going to catch a train."

This brought on a long discussion of the many deprivations they had to suffer in the temporary quarters. It
seemed that boys in the other part of the home were
provided with towels and sheets, as well as with books
and games and radios. But after some inmates of the
temporary dormitory had tried to hang themselves with
the linens and had attempted to set fire to the place by
burning books and magazines, everything but the walls
and the bunks had been removed. "The only way Specks
could let us have anything would be by staying here to

see that we used it right. And he hasn't got time for that."

Randy and Bobbie listened to all that was said. They found that Specks was the young man who had charge of them during the day. The old man who had brought them up to the dormitory was the "night man" and was called "Wheezy." The biggest and oldest boys of the group were Buster and Spider, who boasted of being nearly seventeen. Next to them were Steve and Al, who were past sixteen, and then came Chris, Jim, and Buddy, who didn't talk much about their age, but who appeared to be the youngest of the group. They all seemed to belong to the same gang, and Buster was evidently the boss.

They left Randy and Bobbie severely alone for the first two weeks of their stay, regarding them as transients until the day Harry came to visit them. Specks had brought them some clean overalls and told them to put them on quickly so they could go down to the office to see their father. They were happy and excited when they left the dormitory, but they were crestfallen when they returned. Both looked as though they might have been crying, but Randy held his head high as he marched up to Buster and asked if he could speak to him.

"We'd like to talk to you about joining the gang."

"Nothin' doing. You kids are just transients and we don't want to have nothin' to do with you."

"But we're not transients any more. Our dad has just told us that our stepmother won't let us come home, not now or ever."

"What did you do?"

"We played hooky, just once."

"The judge won't commit you for playing hooky once."

"Maybe not, but Harry's going to put us in boarding school. We don't want to go to school in vacation."

The big boys gathered round them and felt sorry for "the kids" when they heard their story. Even the toughest shed a tear when Bobbie told how the policeman had killed Pal and how mean their stepmother had been to them.

It was agreed that Randy and Bobbie had enough grievances against the world to entitle them to membership in the gang. They did their best to prove themselves worthy of belonging to the group. But the monotonous routine of the detention home made the days drag slowly for all of them. Each day was like the one before. There was nothing to look forward to except the unappetizing meals and the one-hour recreation period.

Breakfast was usually much the same as the one Randy and Bobbie had had on their first morning. They knew Specks was supposed to take them down to the dining room for lunch, but he brought the meal up to them because that was easier than standing guard while they were eating downstairs. He did take them down to the yard for the hour of exercise which was their recreation —marching up and down in the hot sun. They never knew whether they were going to get supper or not. Old Wheezy was the one who had to bring it, and he didn't like to climb the stairs.

After supper, there was nothing to do but lie around and talk about what they would do when they got out. They varied the monotony by experimenting with each other's bodies, and although Randy and Bobbie had always thought such practices to be nasty, they often participated rather than be considered spoil sports. They also did many other things which they knew to be wrong

but which seemed to be justified by the way they had
been treated.

The big boys were genuinely surprised when "the
kids" handed over a pile of cigarettes they had saved
from recreation periods. "Don't you know you're supposed to give the cigs back if you don't smoke them
before exercises are over?" "Yes, and we know it's all
right to keep them, just so you don't get caught." The
boys slapped them on the back and said they were "learning fast," as indeed they were.

None of the boys thought they had any cause to be
thankful for the frequent showers which kept the weather
fairly cool during the first weeks of June and which often
gave Specks an excuse for cutting out the recreation period. Those who had been in "temporary" before had
never stayed there during the hot summer months; they
had no idea of what was in store for them when the rains
suddenly stopped.

The temporary quarters, on the top floor of the building, were designed to be escape-proof. The architects
had eliminated the ugly iron bars suggestive of prison,
substituting windows which looked like ordinary opaque
glass, but which were unbreakable and immovable.
Heavy iron grills, installed in the ceiling to provide venti-
lation, acted like funnels through which a steady stream
of torrid heat poured into the room. The hot summer
sun beat down on the roof for ten or twelve hours every
day, and since there was no way for the heat to escape
at night, it built up to a new intensity with each day that
passed.

The boys felt as though they were in a furnace con-
suming their bodies and searing their minds. Their
throats were so parched that they could hardly speak

above a whisper. Their stomachs refused to retain food
or water. They tossed feverishly in their bunks, and the
sleep which came to them brought no rest.

Buster knew that some of them were quite sick, but
he delayed reporting their condition to Specks; none of
them wanted to be sent to the infirmary. "It's better to
try to stick it out than to get separated." But they realized that they needed help when Spider and Al were
seized with such violent chills that their teeth were chattering and their iron bunks were shaking.

Specks had just left the breakfast, and he wouldn't be
back again until lunch time. An emergency bell was their
only means of summoning aid, and though forbidden to
use it except in case of fire, they rang it again and again.
When there was no response to their SOS, they concluded
that nobody was concerned about what happened to
them. "We could be burned to a crisp for all they care."

They were wishing they had some covering to put over
the shivering boys, when Randy remembered a story he
had read about a man in the Arctic who had saved another man's life by warming him with the heat of his
body. The suggestion was eagerly accepted. Steaming
bodies were piled on top of Spider and Al until the chills
had subsided.

Buster still intended to ask Specks for a doctor, but he
changed his mind when he caught sight of the two boys
who were brought up with the lunch. Neither he nor
the other boys gave any sign of recognition until after
Specks had left the dormitory. Then pandemonium broke
loose. Randy and Bobbie were at a loss to understand
what it was all about. "Look who's here!" "Hi, Pete!
Hi, Joey!" "If we'd knowed you was coming, we'd 've
baked a cake!" "What's the matter with your friend in

court? Did he go back on you?" Pete and Joey had been members of the gang at the time they got into trouble. The probation officer had paroled them to their parents pending the hearing of the case.

"That double-crossing probation officer is no friend of ours. Know what he did? He coaxed us into spilling everything by letting us believe we'd get off with probation. And when our case came up this morning, he told the judge we weren't 'suitable' for probation because we're 'recidivists' and he don't have the time to watch us close enough."

"Well how come you're here, if your case got tried already?"

"We're just overnight guests. But don't you worry about losing our company. You'll be with us when we get shipped up to the state school tomorrow."

"How do you know that?"

"We heard the 'P.O.' making your reservations, and he promised the superintendent you'd be committed tomorrow morning and delivered to the school not later than ten o'clock tomorrow night."

The boys indulged in earsplitting cuss words. Buster let them rave and rant for a while before he told them they'd have to "pipe down" and do some hard thinking if they wanted to save their skins. Then he turned to Randy and Bobbie and asked them what they wanted to do. "We've got to get out of here before tomorrow morning, but you kids don't have to come."

"You said we could belong to the gang."

"Sure I did, but you might be better off staying here."

"We don't want to stay here, and we don't want to go to boarding school."

"Okay then, but you might be in for some rough stuff if you go with us."

"We don't care. We can take it."

Nickey said that the first thing they were going to have to figure out was how they were going to get hold of their clothes. "We couldn't get any further than the corner in this underwear."

This set them off again on the right of the home to take their clothes away from them. Buster said it was no use to waste time talking about that. "You know they take our clothes to keep us from running away. What we've got to do is to outsmart them by thinking up some way of keeping the coveralls after we come up from the two o'clock exercises."

Collecting these uniforms was the last thing Specks did before he was off for the day. The boys knew that he was very impatient about anything that delayed his departure. Bobbie volunteered the information that Specks tried to save time by leaving his keys in the office on his way upstairs. "How much time can he save by doing that?" "One or two minutes, maybe, but you know every second is precious to Specks."

Nickey said this gave him an idea. "Bobbie can lag behind when we're coming upstairs after recreation this afternoon. He can give us a signal if Specks stops to leave his keys in the office. Then we'll pretend that we're running a race and we'll get into a scuffle when we're at the top of the stairs. The prop holding the dormitory door open will be knocked out 'accidentally on purpose,' and we'll let the door slam shut before Specks can get in. He may go down and get his keys and come back for the coveralls. If he does, we're all washed up. But we'll have to pray that he won't."

Specks didn't notice anything unusual about the boys that afternoon, except that they lingered in the yard for several minutes after he had rung the bell for them to stop marching. They proceeded to the stairway in an orderly manner after he rang the bell a second time, and they didn't break ranks until after he had stepped into the office to turn his keys over to the night man. He heard a slight rumpus at the top of the stairs and he hurried up to see what it was about, but the dormitory door had slammed shut before he reached it.

The boys were elated over having won the first round in their fight for liberation. Pete produced a watch he had managed to conceal on his person when he was searched. If it hadn't been for this watch, the boys would have thought that every minute was an hour. When it was half past three, they knew that they were safe as far as Specks was concerned, because they were sure that he wouldn't work a half-hour overtime on any account.

They guessed that he had told Wheezy to collect the coveralls. Although they didn't think the old man would make a special trip up the stairs for them, they held themselves in readiness throughout the long, hot afternoon.

An hour before sundown the big lights came on, increasing the temperature of the dormitory, and the thick khaki uniforms tortured the boys' bodies almost beyond endurance, but their young hearts were filled with hope which could not be stifled by either heat or delay.

The iron door shut them off from all sounds as effectively as though they were in another world, and they had no warning of Wheezy's approach until his key was in the lock. He had some difficulty in getting the door open, and he seemed more winded than usual as he told the boys to take off their coveralls and give them to him. When they made no move to obey him, he took his keys from the door and walked into the room very slowly. He was panting as though he had been running. He didn't make the slightest resistance when the boys surrounded him and took the keys.

They had intended to lock him in the bathroom, but he looked so tired and harmless that they led him over to one of the bunks and told him to lie down and keep quiet. They were halfway down the stairs before Nickey thought about the emergency bell and ran back to disconnect it so that Wheezy couldn't sound any alarm. But he told the boys that he needn't have bothered about it because the old man was already fast asleep.

In a matter of minutes they unlocked the outside door of the office and let themselves out into the brightly lighted yard. Their first impulse was to run as fast as they could. Then Buster whispered to them to lie down and crawl along the ground on their bellies. He didn't let them stand up until they were well past the last of the numerous buildings of the detention home. Then he told them to break up into small groups and walk along as though they weren't going anywhere in particular.

They did as they were told. Some of them looked up and marveled at the star-studded sky. Randy said he couldn't remember ever having seen so many stars before. "I reckon you don't notice the stars so much until you've been locked up in a place where you can't see them," Chris said. Pete was glad there was no "lousy moon" to show them up and make targets out of them. He asked Buster if he didn't think it was safe to begin "putting on a little speed." But Spider and Al were still too weak to walk very fast, and they begged the others not to get too far ahead.

Pete announced that it was eleven o'clock. They knew then that they had been walking for more than an hour and should have reached the highway by this time, if they hadn't taken the wrong direction when they left the home. They were afraid to retrace their steps, and yet they knew it would take them twice as long to get out of the city by the circuitous route they would now have to take.

There seemed to be only one way out of their desperate situation; that was to "borrow" a car. Pete and Joey were supposed to be the experts on starting cars without keys, but they failed on the first one they tried. They thought they were on the point of succeeding with the next one, when the lights went on in a nearby residence and frightened all the boys out of their wits. They took to their heels and didn't stop running until they were quite sure no one was following them. They didn't even look at another car until they spied an old jalopy in front of a vacant lot. Buster said it was probably "hot," but when he found that it was rigged so as not to require a key, he thought it might be their best bet. He took the wheel, telling Spider and Al to sit in front with him and let the others pile into the back.

The car was minus a top, but this only added to the boys' enjoyment. They felt as though they were flying away from the walls which had confined them, into a new world, where they would be free as the wind which blew against their faces.

Riding along with no particular destination in mind, they came to an intersection where several highways converged. They saw by the signs that they could get out of the state very quickly by heading for Mississippi. To reach the Texas border, they would have to travel many miles, but they unhesitatingly chose the road which led to the Lone Star State—the land of all their dreams.

Buster stepped on the gas, and although there was no speedometer to tell them how fast or how far they were traveling, they were satisfied that they were moving at what was top speed for the "old crate." If they could keep it up, they would have a head start of several hundred miles before they were even missed from the home.

The engine performed very well for nearly two hours. Then it started to balk and sputter. Buster pulled out the primer, muttering, "She was running good, and now she won't pick up." He shifted gears and gunned the accelerator, but the motor continued to hiccup. Finally it gave one last gasp and died.

They jumped out of the car and raised the hood, but it was too dark for them to see anything. After several of them had taken turns at the wheel without being able to get as much as a "chirp" out of the engine, Nickey found a stick and plunged it into the gas tank. The stick came up dry as a bone, and there was nothing for them to do but push the car out of the traffic lane and start walking.

The darkness seemed to be growing more intense. When they could no longer see the white line down the middle of the road, Buster said they might just as well stop and wait for daylight. Steve offered to stand watch and let the rest of them get a little sleep, and he promised to wake them up at the first crack of dawn.

They lay down by the side of the road. It seemed to them that they had hardly closed their eyes, when Steve awakened them with a very good imitation of the gong in the detention quarters. Then he pretended that he was Specks bringing up their breakfast. They all said, "No, thank you, we'd rather be hungry out here than eating that slop in the home."

Soon it was light enough for them to see their way. They trudged along singing snatches of songs and whistling tunes that came into their heads. They wondered why more people didn't get up early enough to see the "gorgeous show" put on by the sun as it rose from below the horizon, changing the gray morning sky into a mass of glowing color.

They couldn't entirely forget their empty stomachs, but they were able to laugh heartily when Steve looked at the endless acres of pine stumps and said he'd be tempted to try eating a couple of them if he had some ketchup. Buster said that transportation was more important than food to them just then, and some of the boys got astride the stumps and went through the motions of riding them.

Nickey was clowning with the rest of them when suddenly he stopped and blinked his eyes. "Do you see what I see, or is that just a mirage up ahead?" He was pointing to an object which turned out to be an old truck lying in a ditch.

Buster said it wasn't exactly what he would have ordered, but they all went to work and managed to get it out of the ditch. The battery was run down, and the tires were worn thin, but a tank half-full of gas encouraged them to try to get it going. They put it in gear and pushed with all their might until the engine gave a sudden cough and started vibrating so violently that it threatened to shake the old body to pieces.

The boys sent up a cheer. As they climbed into the back of the truck, Buster said that Spider and Al and Randy and Bobbie had better ride in the cab with him so as not to get sun-struck. Nobody questioned his decision or doubted he was looking out for the ones who needed attention.

The truck made so much noise that Nickey had difficulty attracting Buster's attention when he saw a building that none of the others seemed to have noticed. It was located on a curving road, which had formed part of the highway at one time, but which had been abandoned for the straight road on which they were traveling. Buster slowed down as soon as he understood what Nickey was saying, and he agreed that it might be a good idea to go over to the building and see what it was. He pulled over to the shoulder of the road and stopped the truck without shutting off the motor.

The building appeared to have been a general store and gas station. It had probably been closed because the road in front of it was no longer used. Nickey didn't think it likely that gas had been left in the tank, but he found a wrench and tried to coax the old pump into action. The other boys were more interested in the contents of the store. They lifted Bobbie on their shoulders so that he could crawl in through a small transom and open the door for them.

Their hearts sank when they went in. The shelves were empty, and everything was covered with a thick layer of dust. But they continued looking until they discovered two unopened cases of canned goods under a back counter and a small box of change in one of the drawers of an old desk.

They ran outside to show Nickey their find and to tell him he could let the old pump alone because they now had money to buy gas. Nickey had the wrench in his hand and he was about to throw it away when Steve stopped him.

"Don't throw it away, Nickey. We've got to have something to open the cans with."

As soon as they were on their way again, Buster told Steve that he was appointed to serve the food. Steve opened first one case and then the other. He was speechless with disappointment when he found that each case contained forty-eight cans of beans. He knew the boys were very hungry, but he also knew that each of them had solemnly sworn never again to look at a bean if they ever got out of the home. Was that why Buster had picked him out for the job?

He didn't feel very funny, but he assumed the most comical expression he could manage, looking at his companions as though he were completely mystified. "How did that store-keeper know that we were on an exclusive bean diet?" Then he handed an opened can to each of the boys with a bow and a flourish, assuring them that the beans "à la fresh air" which he was serving with a delicious "hunger sauce" would not taste anything like beans "à la detention home."

For the first time in many weeks, the boys ate their fill without feeling any pangs of illness or nausea. Then some of them lay back and tried to go to sleep, with the sun blazing down in their faces as though it were trying to keep them from missing the bright lights of the detention dormitory.

But Nickey couldn't relax. He was still worried about their gas supply. He kept a sharp lookout for filling stations, calling out every time he saw one. But Buster sped past all of them. When he did stop, it was not in front of a station.

He asked Nickey to "hop out" and check the gas. He didn't seem surprised when he heard it was "practically out." "That's just about what I figured. But it would be taking too much of a chance to drive into a filling station. The home must have broadcast our disappearance by now, and it wouldn't be hard for anybody to identify twelve juveniles all dressed in khaki coveralls."

Buster said he was going to walk back to the last station they had passed. He asked for a volunteer to go with him. When all the boys held up their hands, he said he wanted only one and that he would take Randy if Bobbie wasn't afraid to stay behind without him. "I guess we'll be back, but you never can tell, and I know you kids have never been separated."

Bobbie made no objection, and Randy felt very important as he strode along beside Buster and tried to hear everything he was saying. "If the station man asks any questions, don't forget that you're my little brother and that we're on our way to our grandmother's place about sixty miles from here. If he has to know who our grandmother is, Smith will be as good a name as any."

The man inside the tiny office attached to the station was so absorbed in listening to a radio program that he didn't see Buster and Randy until they were standing in the doorway. He was startled by their sudden appearance, and he looked at them suspiciously when they asked if they could borrow a can to carry some gas to their car. "Where's your car?"

Buster answered that it was "down the road a piece." He took a handful of change from his pocket and displayed it. "We've got money to pay for it, Mister."

"Yes, I see you have. Well, this here little can will

hold enough to get your car here, if it's down the road
like you say."

Buster tried to persuade him to let them have a larger
can by telling him that it was "damn hard" to start their
"old bus" even once, "much less twice." The man didn't
like the looks of Buster, and he was on the point of telling
him to go away and stop bothering him when Randy
pointed to a big five-gallon can. "Could we have that
one, please sir?" he asked timidly. There was something
appealing about the boy's face and manner, and the man
didn't have the heart to refuse him. "Oh, all right, I
guess you can have it."

The radio was still blaring out its syncopated noise
when the man put the hose nozzle into the can. Just as
he was turning on the pump the program was interrupted
for "an important announcement." There were a few
moments of silence. Then a loud, jubilant voice rang out
over the air. "Here's the news we've been waiting for,
and I'm sure you'll agree that it was well worth the slight
delay. The elderly attendant at the Boys' Detention
Home here in the city was found dead this morning, and
the twelve juveniles who escaped from the temporary
quarters of the home are wanted for his murder."

The last words were spoken very slowly. Each syl-
lable was enunciated with exaggerated clarity, as though
to make sure that listeners would be properly impressed.
Even so, Buster and Randy found it hard to believe their
ears until the station man dispelled all doubt by his excited exclamations. "What d'you know about that! A
bunch of kids have gone and murdered an old man!
They're gonna haf to do somethin' about them juvenile
delinquents! They're gettin' worse every day!"

The overflowing gas can distracted his attention for

a moment, and he ran to the pump to turn it off. But he still seemed to be deeply immersed in thought as he held out his hand. "That'll be a dollar and eighty-six cents."

Buster dropped eight quarters into the outstretched palm, and he was going off without the gas when the man called to him in a rough voice. "You come back here, Buddy." His heart leapt into his throat. He turned around to look for Randy. The station man caught him by the arm. "Not so fast. You go back there and help your little brother with that can. It's too heavy for him."

Buster breathed a sigh of relief and tried to act the part of the "bossy" big brother until they were out of the man's sight and hearing. "That was a close shave, Randy, but you did all right."

The boys knew that something must have gone wrong when Buster returned to the truck and told all of them to get in the back while he was pouring the gas into the tank. "All but you, Spider. Maybe you could take the wheel if you feel all right."

"I'm okay now. But what's up?"

Buster ignored the question until after he made all of them lie down flat in the back of the truck and told Spider to drive "like hell."

When Buster told them about the announcement, their first reaction was one of incredulous indignation. "You mean they're trying to pin a murder rap on us!" "They can't accuse us of killing old Wheezy!" "We didn't hurt him!" "Why, we never even touched the old buzzard!"

Buster let them talk themselves out before he spoke. "Let's get this straight. We all know that the only crime we committed was running away from the home. We've got to remember that and to keep on remembering it if any of us get caught. And just to make sure that we don't forget it, let's raise our right hands up to God and swear that we won't let nobody trick us into confessing that we killed the old man."

After they had taken the oath, a strange silence fell over them. Steve tried to distract them with the mimicry which usually delighted them, but their hearts were heavy with fear and foreboding. Consciousness of their innocence gave them little confidence in their ability to vindicate themselves. Each had tasted the bitter cup of human injustice. Peter, who had had more experience with the police and the courts than any of them, expressed what was in all their minds when he said, "It looks like the cards are stacked against us."

Their need to escape was more urgent than ever now; they were convinced that there was no hope for them if they were caught. Spider drove like mad when he was on the open road, but he was careful to by-pass the main streets of the towns through which they had to pass. The boys ducked every time they saw a pedestrian or another vehicle, and they watched the highway signs anxiously, hoping against hope that their gas would hold out until they reached the state line.

No one attempted to stop them. When trouble came it was from an unexpected quarter. It hadn't occurred to any of them that the hot pavement and the speed at which they were traveling would build up more air pressure than the worn tires of the truck could withstand.

Spider said the blowout took the wheel right out of his hand. The truck careened into a ditch and turned over before he could do anything to prevent it.

All the boys were shaken up and scared, but Bobbie seemed to be the only one who was badly hurt. The truck was a complete wreck, and Buster said the boys would have to "hoof it" the rest of the way. Since it wasn't safe for them to walk along the highway, they would have to head for some thick woods in the distance.

First, they had to do something about Bobbie. Buster became very serious after he had examined him and discovered the extent of his injuries. "The kid's in bad shape. His left leg's broken in two places and the bone is sticking out through the flesh. He might lose his leg if we don't get him to a doctor right away."

Randy wanted the others to go on, but the big boys insisted on carrying Bobbie to the gate of a farmhouse. They then turned him over to Randy and set out for the woods. After they were out of sight, Randy went into the house and asked the farmer to take his brother to the nearest doctor.

The farmer didn't have a car, but he immediately hitched up his horse and wagon and made Bobbie as comfortable as he could. He put a piece of wood under his leg, telling Randy to try to hold it still if they hit any bumps in the road.

Randy and Bobbie decided that farmers were "nice people" because they tried to help you without doing a lot of talking about it. After they arrived at the doctor's, they felt the same way about country doctors.

All the doctors they had ever known asked a lot of "silly questions" before they tried to do anything for you. But this country doctor just lifted Bobbie from the wagon and carried him to a table in his office without saying a word. Then he cut away the khaki coverall and started wiping the dirt and grime from the injured leg. When he saw that the slightest touch was painful to Bobbie, he gave him a hypodermic and waited until it had taken effect before he resumed his work. He pressed the protruding bones into place and splinted and bandaged the leg without assistance. Not until he had finished the job did he turn to Randy and ask, "Where are you boys from?"

If he had asked the question earlier, or if he had been less considerate of Bobbie, Randy might have been able to lie to him. As it was, he looked him straight in the eye and answered, "We're from New Orleans. But we don't ever want to go back there."

The doctor was evidently a little puzzled at this. "Mind telling me where you want to go?"

"We were on our way to Texas."

"All by yourselves?"

Randy wanted to be honest with the doctor, but he couldn't answer this last question without involving the other boys, and so he asked the doctor how long it would be before Bobbie would be able to walk.

The doctor said that would all depend and carried Bobbie to a couch in the next room. After treating a few more patients, he looked in on the boys and saw that Bobbie was sleeping peacefully and that Randy was lying on the floor beside him.

He closed the office door without locking it. Then he went home and did something he regretted for many years. He meant no harm to the boys, but he suspected that they had run away from a good home and that their parents were probably worried about them; he telephoned the New Orleans police and asked for a description of any boys who were missing from their homes. The police replied that their list of runaways was so long that it would be impossible to read it over the telephone. They suggested that the doctor describe any boys who may have looked suspicious.

This threw a different light on the matter. The doctor decided that he would want to talk to the boys again before he determined whether or not it was his duty to report them to the police, but he had hardly hung up the telephone when it rang again with an insistence which he always recognized as long distance. It was the New Orleans police calling him back and wanting to know if he had seen any boys dressed in khaki coveralls.

"Yes, I saw two of them."

"Only two? Where are they now?"

"They're right here. I'll keep them until their parents come for them."

"Their parents don't want them, but we want them real bad."

"What do you want them for?"

"For murdering an old man. Will you get the sheriff to hold them for us?"

"I'll hold them, but they can't be the boys you want."

He was even more convinced that they weren't the boys who were wanted for murder when he went back to the office and looked at them again. Asleep, their faces had more of the angelic than the criminal about them. He wondered what had driven them from their home, and he wished with all his heart that he could help them find their way back.

It was nearly morning when the police arrived. The doctor was with them, and he was amazed to find them preparing to take the boys away without having asked them a single question.

"How do you know they're the boys you want, officers?"

"We'd know them uniforms anywhere, Doc."

"But you didn't even ask their names!"

"It's no use asking kids like them anything. They won't answer you, and if they do, they always lie."

The doctor was concerned about Bobbie's leg. "He really shouldn't be moved until the bones have had a chance to set."

"Don't you worry about him, Doc. These kind of kids are tough."

"His bones are no different from those of any other child his age."

"We have to take him, but we'll stretch him out on the back seat and do our best not to hurt him."

They put Randy in between them on the front seat, and they plied him with questions. At first they were casual and friendly. Then they resorted to threats and intimidation. When Randy still refused to talk, they tried an approach which seldom failed. "You think you're smart, but you're just dumb. Your buddies have already confessed everything, and you're going to be left holding the bag if you don't come clean with us."

Bobbie, gradually recovering from the effects of the sedative the doctor had given him, pricked up his ears when he heard the officers talking about the confession. "They even identified the murder weapon. It was an old wrench and you forgot to take it when you left the truck in the ditch."

Randy remained silent, but Bobbie was too horrified to let such a statement go unchallenged. "That's a lie. We never found the wrench until the day after we left the home. And we only used it to open cans."

"So you admit you were members of the murder gang!"

"We don't admit nothing, excepting that we hate policemen. And when we get big, we're going to kill every policeman we meet, just like they killed our dog."

The officers looked at the helpless child and laughingly remarked, "Look who's talking."

They didn't have anything more to say until they had arrived in the city and were taking Bobbie into the hospital. Randy pleaded with them to let him go with his brother.

"He's just a kid, and he gets scared when he's by himself."

"Oh, yeah? Well he didn't seem very scared when he was telling us off just now."

"Maybe he didn't mean everything he said. I guess his leg's hurting pretty bad."

"Now that you've found your tongue, are you ready to do some talking?"

"No, I'm not."

"Not even if we promise to bring you back to stay with your brother?"

"Your promises aren't worth anything. Goodbye, Bobbie, and don't cry."

They took Randy to the District Attorney's office, introducing him as "one of those kids that's wanted for murder." Everybody in the office seemed too busy to acknowledge the introduction, and the officers were perturbed by the apparent indifference. "Ain't anybody around here interested in law enforcement? We travel a thousand miles to pick up a kid that's wanted for murder, and you guys won't even look up when we bring him in."

A young man at one of the desks continued to check some papers as he answered. "We don't want any kids for murder. If you're talking about the case of that old man at the home, that's one we don't have to bother about. The coroner's jury returned a verdict of death through natural causes. There wasn't a scratch or bruise on his body, and his own doctor had told him to stop climbing stairs more than three years ago."

After some profane language directed at everybody in general, the policemen started to leave without Randy, but the young man called them back. "Get that boy out of here. We've got nothing to do with juveniles."

The officers had been on duty all night. Now, instead of being able to deposit Randy in the district attorney's office as they had expected, they had to drive him all the way out to the detention home. They found Specks, seated behind the desk in the office, too absorbed in the book he was reading to give the policemen any attention. "Here's another one that won't raise his head to see what we're bringing him. Take a look, brother. It's one of your own runaways. If you'd lock these kids up a little better we wouldn't have to go chasing all over the country after them."

They were leaving without waiting for a reply, when Specks called to them. "Wait a minute. If this is one of those twelve boys who escaped from temporary quarters, we're not going to take him back."

"Well, that's just too bad. What do you expect us to do with him? Put him in our pocket?"

Specks opened his mouth to answer. When he saw that the officers were already outside the door, he spoke to Randy instead. "You can't stay here. I have orders not to take any of the escapees back."

"Then I can go?"

"I don't know. I guess if I can't let you stay here, I have to let you go. But maybe I should look at your card. What's your name, boy?"

Randy gave his name. He saw that Specks was keeping one eye on the clock as he thumbed through the box of cards. Same old Specks, thought Randy, as though he had been away from the home for a few years instead of a few days. Then he saw him pull out a card and begin talking, either to himself or to some invisible third person. "Oh, here we are! He and his brother were brought in by the police at night, and no case was ever filed against them. I wonder why we let them stay here for six weeks? Oh, I see now. Their father is a minister, and he was trying to find a boarding school for them. What a coincidence! He found a school and was coming for them the very day they ran away!"

Specks picked up the telephone and dialed a number. He asked for the minister. Frances must have answered and said that he wasn't home but that she would give him a message. "Will you please tell him that one of his boys has been returned to the detention home and that we can't keep him. He'll have to come get him right away."

All the old love for his father came crowding back in Randy's heart as he waited to be reunited with him. When Harry finally arrived, Randy rushed into his arms and felt like a little boy again. It was just as if he had never had a stepmother named Frances, or played hooky from school, or joined up with a gang from the detention home. He was sobbing for pure joy—when he thought of Bobbie, who was such an important part of all the remembered happiness. "Bobbie's in the hospital, Daddy. And he must be awful lonesome. Let's go to him right away."

But Harry said there wouldn't be time. He had a taxi waiting outside, and they would have to hurry to catch a train. "They won't let you stay here, and I don't know what I'd do with you if we missed that train."

On the way to the railroad station he took a pair of shoes and a coat from a bag and told Randy to put them on. It was the first time Randy had ever put shoes on dirty, sockless feet, but he made no protest. Nor did he complain about having to put the coat over the heavy coveralls. He thought his father was going to make the journey with him, and he knew a minister's son had to look presentable.

But when Harry put him on the train and asked the conductor to look after him and see that he got off at the right station, he broke down completely. "You aren't going to send me away without letting me talk to you, are you Daddy? There's so much I have to tell you that you don't know about . . ."

"Good-bye, son, and God bless you."

The train was already moving, and Harry jumped off and turned to wave to the small figure standing on the steps. He saw that Randy's arms were stretched out toward him in an imploring gesture, and he could hear his piteous cry above the noise of the station. "Please, Daddy, I'll be good. I promise I'll be good, if you'll just let me stay with you."

The conductor, who came to close the door, spoke kindly to the weeping boy. "Don't cry, son. You'll probably like the boarding school after you get used to it."

Randy dried his eyes on his sleeve and seemed suddenly to be transformed from a pathetic child into a defiant youth. "I won't stay there long enough to get used to it."

"You're not going to run away, after your father taking all the trouble to send you there?"

"I've got to wait for my brother, because he'd never be able to find me if I left before he came."

He had to stay in the boarding school much longer than he had expected because Bobbie's discharge from the hospital was delayed by complications which set in as a result of the long ride in the police car. But Randy never got used to the school. On the contrary, he hated it more with each day that passed. He had the escape plans all mapped out and ready when Bobbie arrived.

The school authorities were at a loss to explain the boys' disappearance. They had attributed Randy's obvious restlessness to his anxiety about his brother. "He was always asking us when Bobbie was coming. And we were confident that he would settle down and get adjusted as soon as his brother got here. It's hard to understand these unstable children."

The members of the gang were interviewed in the state reform school. They told what they knew about the boys, but they denied any knowledge of their whereabouts. "We never saw them after the day the truck crashed and Bobbie's leg got broken. We got caught that same day, and the cops tried to tell us the kids had squealed on us. But we knew better than that. Them kids are okay, and if we ever get out of here, we'll try to find them because they're kinda small to be out on their own. Will we tell them their father wants them to come home? You can bet your life we won't. Why? Because it would just be the same thing all over again if they went back. Maybe you don't know it, but anything's better than being shut up in a place where you don't want to be —like we are."

It was a long time before Harry gave up hoping that his boys would return. He prayed for them as he had never prayed before, and he instituted a nation-wide search. But no trace of them was ever found. They seemed to have vanished just as completely as though the earth had opened up and swallowed them.

6

WHITE ANGEL

The big courtroom which we used as a waiting room was jammed with the usual Monday morning crowd. Seats nailed together in rows in order to conserve space were filled, and many people were standing in the doorway and in the hall.

One mother, who had brought all nine of her children "to show them to the Judge," was scolding them in a loud voice. Another woman was trying to quiet two crying babies in her arms, while two smaller children were tugging at her skirts and yelling lustily. A little girl, just beginning to walk, lost her balance as she toddled down the aisle and gave a piercing scream as her head hit the marble floor. Older children were quarreling about soft drinks and candy bars, and men and women were shouting to make themselves heard above the din.

All the people seated were facing the front of the room; none saw Angel when she entered. The men standing in the doorway stepped aside to let her pass, but they hardly glanced at the child. She walked quickly up the aisle and had reached the low railing at the far end of the room when a large black Negro limped through the

door on a wooden leg. The Probation Officer opened a
small gate in the railing and led Angel to the door of the
Hearing Room as a loud murmur went through the crowd.
"It's her. It's Angel. And that's the nigger."

Excitement ran high. People forgot their own troubles for the moment. Women who had been elbowing
each other disagreeably now began telling the different
versions of the story they had heard about Angel. Before long they were arguing violently, contradicting each
other and themselves. All felt qualified to predict the
outcome of the case, but they "would have given anything" to be able to see what was going on behind the
closed doors of the Hearing Room. In spite of differences of opinion on other subjects, they agreed on one
thing. "It's just disgusting the way you can't never hear
nothing that goes on in this Court."

To those of us who were behind the closed door, there
was nothing exciting or thrilling about the story we had
to hear. Looking at the child, we could see why she had
been called "Angel." The wide, blue eyes, the pure white
skin, and the halo of golden blond hair suggested nothing that was earthly.

She was thirteen years old. If she had been less than
twelve, the charge would have been "rape," and the case
would have been lodged in the Criminal Court. Under
our law, a girl of twelve is legally presumed to be in-
capable of giving her consent to sexual intercourse.
Therefore it is immaterial whether she actually did give
her consent or not. If the girl is over twelve, the sexual act
does not constitute rape unless it is proved that it was
committed without her consent and against her will.
Angel had steadfastly refused to testify that the Negro
had used force in perpetrating the act he committed

against her or that she had resisted him. She was also unwilling to testify that any of the acts had been committed before she reached her twelfth birthday.

This was a matter of great disappointment to the District Attorney, who had no prejudice or feeling of any kind against the Negro, but who was ambitious to build up a record for himself. The District Attorney can never expect his office to be a steppingstone to the governor's mansion unless he wins public acclaim for a number of successful prosecutions in sensational cases. Convictions in rape cases are notoriously hard to get because of the death penalty. Angel's case contained all the elements which would assure wide publicity; and the fact that the perpetrator of the crime was a Negro, and the victim a child, would make it a "push-over" to get a conviction.

The District Attorney thought that he could cover himself with glory if Angel would testify to what everybody believed to be the truth. He talked to her very gently at first, and then he tried being stern and severe, but in the end he had to abandon the rape charge. There was nothing to be gained by a conviction of "carnal knowledge," and so he transferred the case to the Juvenile Court. In this way Angel was saved the mortifying experience of having to take the witness stand in the large Criminal Court, in the presence of a gaping crowd of curiosity-seekers, newspaper reporters, and photographers.

It was bad enough for her to have to appear in our small Hearing Room, with the Judge, the stenographer, the Probation Officer, the District Attorney assigned to the Court, and the defendant and his counsel.

Angel was the only witness. Our District Attorney opened by stating that he would try to handle the case in accordance with what he knew to be the Court's opinion,

that the child was far more important than the case. He
had his duty to perform in prosecuting the defendant,
but as far as he could he would spare the child embarrassment. He was willing to let Angel tell her story in her
own way and without interruption, if that was agreeable
to counsel for the defendant. The attorney for the defendant agreed, reserving his right to cross-examine Angel
when she had completed her direct testimony.

There was no witness stand in our Hearing Room. We
were on one side of a large table, and the District Attorney and Angel sat opposite us. "Nappie," which was the
name by which the Negro was called throughout Angel's
testimony, and his attorney were at one end of the table,
and the stenographer and the Probation Officer were at
the other end.

The District Attorney asked Angel if she was ready
to tell the Court everything that had happened. She
nodded and swallowed very hard. We asked her if she
would like to have some water before she began. She
took the glass we handed her, but hardly touched it with
her lips before putting it down in front of her. She raised
her right hand and swore "to tell the truth, the whole
truth, and nothing but the truth."

She asked if it would be all right if she went "all the
way back" so that she could explain how things had always been for her. We looked at the defendant's lawyer,
and we said it might be easier for Angel if she could begin in this way, even though much of what she said
should prove immaterial and irrelevant to the issues being tried. The lawyer had a short, whispered conversa-
tion with his client and then announced, "Counsel for defendant will interpose no objection."

Angel showed no emotion when she spoke of her parents, but she did choke up with tears when she mentioned Eddie, her little brother, and her sisters, Susie and Ann.

She had nothing to say about her father, except that he deserted the family when her little brother was still a baby. She was seven years old at the time, one of her sisters was four, and the other was three. Her mother, who had worked before the baby was born, went back to work after the father left the home. Angel looked after the children during her mother's absence, but her mother did most of the "real hard work" after she came home in the evening. They lived in a small apartment in the French Quarter. It was convenient to the restaurant in which the mother worked as a waitress, but Angel wished that it was elsewhere, so that the children could have a yard to play in. It was apparent that, even at the age of seven, Angel never considered herself a child. She was the nurse and cook and housekeeper for her little brother and her younger sisters, and she frequently referred to them as "my children." She made no attempt to praise herself for anything she had done for them, for it was evident that everything she did for them was a labor of love.

Her mother's earnings were sufficient to pay the rent and buy food and some clothing, but there was never anything "left over," and when her mother became ill, she had to go to the clinic at Charity Hospital. After several visits, she came home one day and told Angel that she would have to go into the hospital for an operation. She borrowed some money from her employer and gave it to Angel, telling her to make out the best she could with it. She asked a neighbor to keep an eye on the children. The day after Angel's mother went to the hospital, the neighbor came in and said that she had died.

Angel was nine years old at the time of her mother's death, but she felt fully capable of looking after the children. When her money ran out, she went to the neighbor and asked where she could get some more for the rent and for food for the children. The neighbor was a poor woman, and she knew that even if she could lend Angel a few dollars, it wouldn't do any good because the authorities wouldn't let four children live alone in an apartment in the Quarter. She told Angel that she knew of an agency "which was very good to children," and Angel didn't object when she said she'd tell them about Angel's little brother and sisters.

A "nice lady" came to see them, and she asked Angel a lot of questions about the children and about any relatives of her father and mother. If there were any relatives, Angel didn't know anything about them, but she did know about the children, and she told the lady all she knew. The lady came back to see her several times and talked to her about "placing" the children. She may have said something about adoption, but Angel didn't even know what the word meant at that time. She never dreamed that the nice lady was planning to take "her children" away from her. She cried bitterly when she was told that the children were going to be placed for adoption with three different families; even then she didn't understand that she wouldn't know where they were and wouldn't be allowed to visit them. When she found this out, she cried more than ever and wouldn't even look at the people the nice lady brought to see her. It was no wonder that none of them wanted to adopt her. The nice lady said she thought that Angel was too old for adoption anyway, and she placed Angel in an institution.

The first home in which Angel was placed was a home for babies and very young children. Angel would have loved to play with them and mother them, but she wasn't even allowed to go near them. All she could do was look at them, and that just made her miss "her own children" the more. She was given to understand that she was in the home only temporarily, until some institution for older children would accept her. She was told to keep out of the way when visitors came because she didn't belong there. But she sometimes watched them admiring the babies and picking out the ones they wanted to adopt, and she wished she were a little baby so that someone would want to adopt her.

She had high hopes when they told her they could get her in another home, because she thought maybe she'd have something to do there, instead of just sitting still all day doing nothing. She was disappointed when she found that she was again in a place where there were no children of her age. This time the girls were all older than she. The uniforms she had to wear were all much too large for her, and she knew she looked funny because the big girls were always teasing her. They were mean to her, too, and they blamed her for everything that happened. The directress was always shaking her finger at her and telling her what was going to happen if she didn't behave better.

She was put in the lowest class in the school of the home, but the teacher didn't know that she had never been to school before. She stayed in the class for two years without learning anything, and then she was given some tests which showed that she couldn't learn and it was no use trying to teach her. The home authorities

said they couldn't keep "a child who couldn't be educated," and the nice lady had to find another place for her.

The next home was larger than either of the other two.
From the outside it looked beautiful. Once again Angel
thought things were going to be better. Once again she
was disappointed. The trouble about her grade placement began all over again. Angel was then eleven years
old and should have been in the sixth grade, but she didn't
even know how to read and write. It was decided that
she couldn't possibly fit into any of the classes in the home
school, but she could take part in "household duties."
All the girls were supposed to take turns in working in
the laundry, cleaning up the dormitories and showers,
setting the tables, and making salads and other simple
dishes in the pantry. Some of the big girls thought they
were "putting it over" on Angel by making her take their
turns, but she didn't mind at all, especially if the work
was in the pantry. She was eager to learn how to make
things to eat, and she was very grateful when Nappie, the
Negro cook, helped her. She "ruined lots of things" at
first, and she might have been punished if Nappie had
told on her. Instead, he always quickly made something
else and told her not to worry—nobody would ever know
the difference.

In spite of all her failures, she didn't get discouraged
because whenever she did something that was halfway
right, Nappie would praise her and say it was fine. It
got so that when they had visitors for lunch or for supper,
and Nappie was asked which of the girls he wanted to
help him in the pantry, he'd always say, "Angel." This
made her feel important, and for the first time since she
had lost her "children" she knew some happiness.

After she learned to make salads and sandwiches "and

easy things like that," Nappie asked her if she would like to learn to make cakes and pies. She was delighted with the idea, but then she remembered that the girls weren't allowed in the kitchen. Nappie said that was just because he didn't want the girls bothering him, but that he was boss in the kitchen and everything he said "went" there. If it didn't, they'd have to get another cook. He said that if he told her she could come in the kitchen, she could, and nobody else had anything to say about it.

Angel admitted that she hadn't been quite sure that she should go without asking permission, but Nappie said "Yes," and she listened to him because she so wanted to learn how to make all kinds of good things.

Nappie taught her everything he knew about making cakes and cookies and desserts of all kinds. Then he showed her how to decorate cakes and how to make pies and fancy pastries. She tried very hard to do exactly as he said, and after a time she was making cookies almost as good as Nappie's. It took her longer to catch on to the cakes and pies, but she never stopped trying, and Nappie never lost patience with her. She finally succeeded so well that when Nappie let her make and decorate a cake for one of the girls' birthdays, the directress called Nappie into the dining room and said it was the best cake he had ever made.

Angel said it was a long time before she and Nappie talked about anything besides cooking, but one day he told her how he had lost his leg. He said he was a little kid and was stealing a ride on a freight train, when he fell in between two cars. The wheels rolled over one of his legs, and it was so badly mashed that it had to be amputated. That was how he came to be a cook instead of a prize fighter like all the rest of his brothers.

Then Angel told him how she had lost "her children," would never be able to see them again, and could never even find out where they were. She found she could talk about them to Nappie without crying, and she told him over and over how cute Eddie was and how everybody stopped to look at Susie and Ann when she dressed them up and took them out for a walk. The nice lady had told her that they all had good homes with rich people, who would send them to college when they grew up. She told Nappie that this was the only thing that made her feel that maybe it was for the best after all, because if they had been put in the home with her they might have grown up like she did, without even knowing how to read and write.

Nappie said he hadn't gone to school much either, but he had spent three years in the Children's Hospital after he lost his leg, and the teacher there had given him lessons every day. He thought it was a shame that a girl like Angel couldn't read and write, and he offered to teach her if she would come to his room at night after supper. Angel thought that if there was anybody from whom she could learn it was Nappie.

Almost every night after that Angel went to Nappie's room back of the kitchen, when the other girls went to "study period." And for the first time in her life, Angel had a teacher who really believed that she could learn. He kept saying that she'd be teaching him before long, and she herself could see that she was making progress. She said she knew he must have been tired "after standing on that wooden peg all day," but he was never too tired to go over her lessons with her.

When she reached this point of her narrative, she looked at the District Attorney and the Court and said she knew everybody would think that he had offered to teach her just to get her to come to his room so that he could "do that" to her. But she knew it wasn't so. He really liked her, and he wanted to help her, and he had been teaching her a long time before he even touched her.

Then Angel put her head down on the table and cried as though her heart would break. We were all waiting for her to go on and at the same time wishing that she didn't have to, when she lifted her head and said, "You know what he did! Don't make me tell it. I can't say the words. But he didn't force me, and I didn't try to stop him."

We looked at the District Attorney, and he said that much as he regretted it, he would have to question Angel to bring out the facts. He was hesitating before beginning an unpleasant and distasteful task, when Nappie stood up and, without consulting his lawyer, said in a broken voice, "I change my plea to guilty."

The stenographer closed her notebook, and the District Attorney was gathering up his papers, when Angel looked up in wonder and asked, "Does that mean it's over, and I won't have to say anything more about it?" "Yes, Angel, it's over and we hope you won't ever have to speak of it or even think of it again. Try to forget it ever happened."

We knew that the forgetting would be the easier for her since she had not been forced to rehearse the sordid details. In the way of most men who commit such crimes, Nappie had not thought of himself as guilty of any great and irremediable wrong against the child. But when he heard Angel tell her story of loneliness and frustration and her final betrayal by the one person who had befriended her, his heart was moved with pity for the innocent child. He knew then that he had harmed her, and he did the only thing he could to spare her further suffering. He abandoned all hope of escaping punishment, when he changed his plea to "Guilty as charged." And who shall say that he did not thereby redeem himself and restore a child's faith in human nature? We thought that he had when we looked at Angel's radiant face as she left the courtroom.

7

"LUCKY LARRY"

The frail, small form of Mary Marty lay white and still on the hospital bed for many weeks as she hovered in the shadow land between life and death. And the fate of Larry Dixon also hung in the balance during all this time, for it depended upon the slender thread of this young girl's life. Larry was over sixteen years of age and under seventeen. If Mary died, Larry would be tried in the Criminal Court for murder; if she lived, he would be turned over to our Court to do what we could, not to him, but for him.

The District Attorney told us that he breathed a sigh of relief the day Mary's name was taken off the "dangerously ill" list, not only because he knew from experience that it is difficult to get a jury to convict a juvenile of murder, but also because he had taken a liking to Larry. He hoped we wouldn't think he had "gone soft" or anything, but Larry was such a normal boy in every way, that he couldn't help comparing him to his own son. His parting remark pointed up our own thinking. "I don't know what you're going to do with him. But I'm glad it's your job and not mine. I wish you luck."

We didn't know then that the subject of our concern had been called "Lucky Larry" ever since childhood. He told us about it himself, not boastfully, but almost humbly. "They call me 'Lucky Larry,' but I never really believed I was lucky before. When I was eleven my bicycle was knocked down by a truck, and everybody said I was 'lucky' I wasn't killed, but I didn't think that was luck, because I knew that I had tilted my bike so that I would fall out of the path of the truck. It was the same way a couple of years afterward when I was at camp and my sailboat overturned in the lake. The two kids who were with me tried to make it to shore, and they were both drowned. I held onto the boat until somebody came to rescue me. I didn't think that was luck either; it was just using good sense. But now I know I'm lucky, because this was a break I didn't deserve. If she had died, I would have been a murderer. My father's lawyers thought they might be able to get me out of it, but I wouldn't have let them try. I was going to take my punishment, and the only luck I was hoping for was that it would be the chair and not life imprisonment."

From the case history on Larry we learned that he was the only child of wealthy parents. His birth had been normal and so had everything about his development, through infancy, childhood, and adolescence. The District Attorney had been impressed by the fact that Larry was such a normal boy, even after knowing about the act he had committed and without having read the case history.

The reports from the psychiatrists who had examined him likewise showed that there was no evidence of psychosis, schizophrenia, psychopathic personality, or any other abnormality. Tests made by psychologists at our request confirmed previous tests made at Larry's school, rating his intelligence ten to twenty points above average.

We asked the case worker to check again to see if there was any repression, rejection, frustration, or other element in the boy's life, but she could find nothing that would account for his sudden outburst of aggression.

The attorneys employed by Larry's father offered to help us in any way they could. They understood it was not our purpose to punish Larry, but our responsibility to protect him and the public from any possibility of his committing other overt acts. They knew that we could reduce these possibilities, or perhaps eliminate them altogether, if we could find out the cause of his behavior; but they were unable to give us the slightest clue. Everything that they knew about the boy—his character and his previous behavior—was irreconcilable with his commission of such an act. They frankly said that they would never have believed that he did it if he had not himself admitted it.

Larry's parents were eager to tell us everything they could remember about the boy's childhood and youth in the hope that we might be able to find significance in some circumstance or event. They had sent Larry to a nursery school until he was six years old, and after that he attended a select private school. His teachers liked him, and he never seemed to have any trouble in getting along with his schoolmates. He was not very studious, but his parents were satisfied if he made passing grades, even though they thought he could have led his classes if he had wished to make the effort. When he was fourteen, he tried out for the football team of his school but injured his knee in practice and never tried again.

Every summer Larry's parents asked him if he would

prefer to take a trip with them or go to camp. They didn't
let him know that they were disappointed when he always chose to go to camp.

Everyone said he was a fine-looking boy, but for a
long time he didn't pay much attention to his personal
appearance. His mother thought he usually looked rather
"sloppy" in spite of the good clothes she bought him, and
she never could get him to go to the "nice teen-age parties" given by her friends for their children. She thought
it best not to press any of these matters as she felt sure
he was "just passing through a phase" and would get along
better if he were let alone.

Shortly before his sixteenth birthday she noticed a
change. He became very particular about his clothes
and accessories and took great pains to look as neat as
possible. She immediately jumped to the conclusion that
he was becoming interested in girls, though she saw no
evidence of it, and he still refused to go to parties.

Larry Dixon's mother never knew where he met Mary,
or when. She admitted that she might not have approved
of Larry's association with her if she had known about it.
Mary was one month younger than Larry. She lived with
her parents in one of the public housing projects, part of
a slum clearance project commonly referred to by its
residents, as well as by the rest of the community, as "The
Slums." Mrs. Dixon said that she knew it was no disgrace to live in "The Slums," and she was sure that lots
of good people lived there. As a matter of fact, she knew
that Mary was a good girl, but she and Larry didn't belong in the same set; and if she had been asked, she would
have said it was better for both of them not to have anything to do with each other.

But she wasn't asked, and Larry therefore couldn't

have known how she felt about Mary, although it was possible that he knew her general ideas about such things. She wanted us to understand that she was telling us this without any thought of proving that she had been right, because she had never had the remotest idea that such a tragedy as this could happen. She was merely trying to be honest, because if her attitude was in any way responsible for what Larry had done, she wanted to take the blame. We listened to all that she had to say and assured her there was nothing to be gained by fixing the blame on anyone.

Like Larry, Mary was an only child. Both her parents were over forty when she was born, and to say that they "idolized" her would be an understatement. In their eyes, she was all that was good and lovely, and they had no other thought but her happiness. They knew when she met Larry, and they knew everything about Larry that Mary knew, for she had no secrets from them. She brought him home to meet them at the first opportunity, and she was glad they liked him and he liked them. She never had to ask if she could go here or there, but she always told her parents where she was going and what time she'd be back. And she told Larry that she made it a point to get home a little before the time she said; she didn't want her father and mother to worry about her. They said they knew she was able to take care of herself, but with so many automobile accidents and "things like that," they might be afraid that something had happened to her if she were late. Larry agreed with her and said he thought her parents were "swell." The girls who went to his school had "punk" parents, who were always nagging them and not trusting them. He thought that some of the girls hated their parents, and he didn't blame them.

Mary's parents didn't think that anything she did could be wrong, and after they knew Larry a while, they felt almost the same way about him. But when Mary told them that Larry never wanted to meet any of her friends, they didn't quite like the idea. They asked Mary if she knew why he didn't care to know her friends, and when she said the only reason he gave was that he wanted her all to himself, her father looked worried. "You're both too young for that. But what about his friends? Have you met any of them?" Mary said, "No," but Larry had shown her where some of them lived when he took her riding in his mother's car. "They all live in beautiful, big houses, with lawns and gardens and fountains, and some of them even have swimming pools."

One day when Larry was walking home from school with her, two boys in a convertible stopped and asked if they could give Larry and Mary a "lift." Larry just answered, "No," without introducing them, and when Mary said she would have liked to ride in the convertible, Larry's only comment was, "I guess I could have one, if I wanted it." Mary thought that any car was wonderful because her folks had never owned one, but she thought a convertible was "just super." When Larry said he could have one if he wanted it, she had asked enthusiastically, "Oh, could you?" She had been a little disappointed when Larry answered, "Yes, but I don't want it."

The subject didn't come up again until Mary mentioned that Arty Williams, the boy who lived in the project apartment next to theirs, had saved up enough money to buy a jalopy and was going to teach her to drive. She remembered afterward that this was the first time Larry had become really angry with her. He didn't know a thing about Arty, but he made a lot of ugly remarks about him, and he talked to Mary in a tone of voice that nobody had ever used to her before. She was too shocked to tell him that he must be a different kind of boy from what she had thought. She was thinking that she never wanted to have anything more to do with him when he apologized and appeared to be so sorry that she promised to forget it. They kissed and made up, and Larry said he was going to ask his parents for a convertible.

Mary found that he was right when he said he could have a car for the asking; less than a week later, he was waiting for her one day when she came out of school, in the "longest, most beautiful convertible" she had ever seen. Larry asked her if she liked the color, saying, "It's 'heavenly blue,' and somehow or another, I thought it looked like you." Mary liked everything about the convertible, and when Larry said he was going to teach her to drive it, she said she would be afraid to learn on a brand new car like that because it would "kill" her if she put so much as a scratch on it.

It was "lots of fun" learning how to drive, and Mary had plenty of practice, because Larry picked her up after school almost every day and let her drive around the park. When Mary was sure she knew how to drive, she asked Larry what he thought of taking her parents for a short ride so they could see how well she handled the car. Larry said, "I've already told them. Won't they take my word for it?" Mary admitted that her real reason was not to show off her driving but to give them a ride because they never went anywhere. Larry said, "O.K. We'll take them sometime," and Mary decided she wouldn't mention it again unless he did.

The following Saturday afternoon, Mary's father and mother were in the living room when Larry came to get Mary. He chatted with them while he was waiting for Mary to get dressed, and when she was ready to go, he asked them very nonchalantly, as though the idea had just occurred to him, if they would like to go for a ride. Mary's father said, "No, thank you, son. But I'm sure some of Mary's friends would be tickled to death to ride in that fancy car of yours."

Larry didn't answer Mr. Marty, and when Mary kissed her father good-bye, she saw that he looked a little put out. She gave him an extra hug and kiss and told him she'd be back in time for "eats." She knew he had got over it when he asked Larry if he'd stay for supper.

As far as Mary could remember, this was the second time that Larry got "very mad at her." Of course she had to "take up for her father." She tried to explain that he had often heard her say that all her friends were "just dying to ride in Larry's swanky convertible" and that her father was just trying "to put in a good word for them." This only made Larry more angry, and he turned on her. Among other horrid things, he said, "I'd thank you not to be talking about me or my car to your friends."

Although she wanted to stop arguing, Mary felt that she had to find out once and for all what was the matter with her friends. She asked Larry why he disliked people he didn't even know and had never met. She was at a loss to understand what he meant by his reply. "I don't want to know them, period." She tried to pursue the subject further, but she succeeded only in exasperating Larry more. He finally stopped the car. "Listen, Mary, I like you, and I like your mother and dad. If that's not enough for you, it's just too bad." She was furious as she answered, "It's not enough," and got out of the car and walked home.

Her mother was very flustered when she came back so early. She said, "Oh, Mary, I'm sorry, I haven't started supper yet." Mary told her it wasn't nearly supper time and that Larry hadn't come home with her. Her father was distressed, and when he said he was sorry if he had caused the trouble, Mary told him it wasn't his fault. She said she had to have a showdown with Larry some time, and this was as good a time as any. Both her parents agreed with everything she said and admitted that they had been worried about the fact that Larry took up all of her time. They knew she enjoyed riding in the convertible, but they thought she would have enjoyed it more if her friends could have gone along sometimes. Mary wasn't selfish, they were sure of that, but they were afraid Larry was making her look selfish to her friends. They also felt that if Larry didn't like her friends, he should introduce her to his and not just monopolize her all the time the way he was doing.

Mary didn't see Larry for a whole week after that. She missed him terribly, and at the same time she felt "sort of relieved." She was very fond of him, but there was something about him that she couldn't understand. She didn't understand herself, either, when she discovered how glad she was to see him the following Sunday. He rang the bell, and when she went to the door, he asked very humbly, "Can I come in?" She answered, "Of course," and she remembered thinking afterward that she wouldn't have had to say anything because "it was written all over my face how glad I was." Her father and mother greeted him politely, and "anybody could see they were trying to be nice." Larry thought they were having to try awfully hard and that they weren't glad that he had come back.

But he knew Mary was, and he wanted her to go for a ride so they could talk things over. When Mary said, "We can talk right here," her father and mother gathered up the papers they had been reading and went to their room.

Larry told Mary how sorry he was for the way he had acted and said he would do anything she asked, if she'd "make up" with him. He said he had "almost gone out of his mind" during the week they had been separated, and he couldn't get along without her. He cried "like a baby" when he told her how he had been unable to eat or sleep since he last saw her. Mary was touched by the fact that he needed her so much, and she wanted to tell him that she had missed him too; but she was a sensible girl, and she realized that it was no use "to make up," only to "fall out" about the same thing. She told Larry that they had to settle it then and there. They talked and talked "without getting anywhere," and then Larry begged her to wait until after Christmas, which was only one week away. She let herself be persuaded because she "really didn't like to quarrel with anybody, and especially not with Larry."

His holidays had already started, and he was leaving the next day with his father for a plane trip to New York. He told Mary that he would be back in a few days, but when he met her the following Thursday afternoon, she could hardly believe that he had been to New York and back since she saw him Sunday. He said jokingly, "I can prove it, because I bought your Christmas present in New York." Mary wanted to see it right away, but he said they would spend the next day, which was Friday, in the country, and he would give it to her in a lovely place he had "all picked out." When Mary told him that her holidays didn't start until Saturday, he said he had thought they began Friday, but anyhow she could "cut" school just for once.

Larry didn't care anything about his school record. It was hard for him to understand why Mary took school so seriously. He wasn't at all impressed by her explanation that someday she was going to have to earn her own living and that she'd have to be "a housemaid or something like that" if she didn't have an education. He now argued that there was never "much doing" the day before the Christmas holidays anyway, and she admitted that this was so and said she'd consider it. She could see that he was trying not to get angry as he asked, "What do you mean, consider it?" She answered that she wanted to ask her parents if they thought that it would be all right, and he almost shouted at her, "Ask your parents if you can cut school? You must be crazy!" She said she couldn't go with him for a trip to the country without telling her parents where she was going, because she had never done anything like that in her life.

They argued about it for a long time, and Larry said he was going to do everything Mary wanted after Christmas, and he was asking her to do this for him. She saw that he had set his heart on it, and she finally agreed to go with him.

He came for her the next morning, just about school time. He was in high spirits and told her how "sharp" she looked in her new outfit. She left him standing at the door and ran into the kitchen to kiss her mother good-bye. When she came back, he had already started out to the car, and he didn't notice the big box she was carrying until she was putting it on the rear seat of the convertible. He hardly glanced at it then because he had to watch his chance to pull out from the curb. He hadn't forgotten it though. After they were on their way, he looked back and asked, "What's that big package? My Christmas present?" Mary said, "No, silly, that's our lunch. Mother fixed it for us." He looked as though he could hardly believe his ears. "Your mother fixed our lunch? Then you must have told her! You promised you wouldn't."

Mary saw that he was very angry. She tried in vain to reason with him, saying she thought the only reason he didn't want her to tell her parents was that he was afraid they wouldn't let her skip school. But she knew that they always saw things her way and that they wouldn't object to anything she really wanted to do. She had been right, and her mother had got up early that morning to make things that Larry liked for their box lunch. Mary still didn't feel quite right about cutting classes, but she couldn't have had any fun at all if she had sneaked off without telling her parents.

When she asked Larry if he didn't want her to have fun on the picnic, he didn't answer. Then she got angry, and she told him that she was sorry she had cut school to please somebody like him. She didn't know how far they had driven, but she knew it was too far for her to walk back. She asked Larry to turn around and take her back home, and she leaned over to look at his wrist watch to see if she could still make it to school. He pushed her away roughly without answering, and then he started to drive faster and faster.

He pressed the accelerator down against the floor board until the hand of the speedometer pointed to 100. He weaved in and out between traffic going in both directions, and he just missed colliding with trucks and vehicles of all kinds. As they went veering past a car that was going almost as fast as they were, they hit a bump in the road and the convertible swayed and tilted as though it was about to overturn. But it righted itself, and they plunged madly on. After each narrow escape, Larry would look at Mary out of the corner of his eye. Her lips were pressed into a firm, tight line, and her hands were clenched, but she wouldn't look at him or talk to him.

In telling about it afterward, Larry said he was determined to make Mary ask him to slow down. He knew she had made up her mind that she wouldn't do it, but he thought he could force her because he could see that she was terribly frightened. He didn't think she could have held out much longer, but as it happened, she won out in the end because he had to take his foot off the accelerator when he heard the siren of the highway patrol behind them. Realizing that he was going too fast to apply the brakes, he turned into a side road, and they bumped along for a distance of about two city blocks before he came to a complete stop.

He was looking back to see if the cop was still following them when he noticed that Mary was trying to get out of the car. He reached over her and held the door shut. "Oh, no, you don't." Then he grabbed her by both shoulders and tried to kiss her. She had let him kiss her many times before, but he knew that she was angry now and didn't want to be kissed. He wanted to force her, more because she didn't want him to than because he really wanted to kiss her. She struggled fiercely and tried with all her might to push him away, and although he was much the stronger of the two, she managed to fight him off for a while. He finally got hold of both her hands and pinned them in her lap and held them there. Then he leaned over her and held her down with one of his knees as he pressed his fingers tightly around her throat.

He didn't know how long he had been choking her when he felt her body suddenly go limp. Then he released his hold, and her head fell back against the seat. He recoiled in horror as he saw that her eyes were popping out of their sockets and her tongue was hanging over her chin. He remembered muttering to himself, "How could I ever have thought she was pretty?" He didn't really come to his senses, however, until she slumped down from the seat with a dull thud. He worked frantically for several minutes, trying to pull her up. When he found that her body was too limp to stay on the seat, he realized what he had done.

Now it was he who was frightened. He was trying to think what he should do when he heard the patrol car turning into the road. He got out and beckoned to the cop and led him toward the convertible, trying to tell him what had happened. But the officer was too excited to listen to him. He was "raving" so much about the speed at which Larry had been traveling that the boy couldn't "get a word in edgeways." He was surprised to find that there was anything left of the convertible, and when Larry pointed to Mary, lying in a small heap on the floor board, his wrath knew no bounds; but he did try to revive the girl with some things he took out of his first aid kit. When she didn't respond, he helped Larry lift her onto the rear seat of the convertible and stretch her out as best they could. Then the cop took the wheel of the car and motioned to Larry to get in the other side. Within half an hour, they were in the emergency room of the hospital, and the officer was doing all of the talking. "This kid was burning up the highway, doing over a hundred and dashing in and out between traffic so as to make anybody's hair stand on end. And then he hears me coming and thinks to outsmart me by swerving into a rough side road. Then he jams on his brakes, and God only knows why they weren't both killed instantly. The girl was already 'out' when I caught up with them, but I don't think she's dead yet."

They took Mary into the examination room on a stretcher, and Larry and the cop were told to go to the desk. Larry gave Mary's name and address, and the cop took over when it came to giving the details of the "accident."

Larry tried to correct him when he said that Mary had struck her head, but the cop glared at him savagely and told him to keep his mouth shut. He said it was a pity it wasn't Larry lying there "at death's door" instead of that poor young girl. Then he grabbed Larry by the arm and said, "And now you're coming with me to the station." Larry said, "All right, Officer, I'll go with you, and you won't have to drag me, but couldn't we find out if she's dead before we go?" The cop thought it over. "Well, maybe it wouldn't be a bad idea at that. Then we'll know what to book you for."

It was nearly an hour before an interne in a white coat came down the hall. They looked at him expectantly, but he brushed past them and went over to the desk. The girl handed him the admission sheet on which she had written down all the details about the "accident" which the cop had given to her. The interne looked at it incredulously and then said, "Impossible! It couldn't have happened that way." The cop stepped up to the desk and once more told the story of how "this crazy kid was speeding along the highway and lost control of his car when he tried to turn into a bumpy road, and jammed on his brakes while he was still going over a hundred." He seemed to have forgotten that he hadn't actually seen the "accident," and he went on talking and supplying details, which could have originated only in his imagination. The interne stopped him. "All right, Officer, have it your way. All I want to know is whether you want to take the fingerprints from the girl's throat before we wash them off."

For the first time since the "accident," the cop was speechless, but Larry answered the question. "You won't have to, they're mine. Is she dead, doctor?"

The interne said she was still alive; but she had no pulse, and respiration was almost imperceptible. When the cop recovered his powers of speech, he said he guessed they'd better get the prints "just in case this young 'punk' tries to say I beat that confession out of him."

Somebody tipped off the newspapers, and there was a gang of photographers and reporters waiting for Larry when he arrived at the station. The photographers had the "first go" at him. He was too dazed and frightened to resist. They pushed him into every possible pose and told him to laugh and then to cry. They took his picture from every angle, and then the reporters took over. First, a girl reporter lay on the floor and asked him to show her "exactly how he did it." They all took turns in shooting questions at him, and he answered willingly, trying to remember every detail. He thought they were "just dumb," and he tried to correct them when they started off questions by misquoting something he had previously said. But when he found that they were deliberately twisting and changing his statements, he asked them how they could expect him to answer right, when their questions were wrong. He endured the torture as long as he could and then cried out in agony, "Can't you guys get together and tell me what it is that you want me to say? No matter what it is, I'll say it, if you'll just let me alone."

But his inquisitors were merciless, and he was no match for them. They continued to ply him with questions, and they goaded him into answering long after he had decided that he would let nobody drag another word from him. They were on the scent of good copy and maybe by-lines, and they were not to be deterred. It is said that even the fiercest bloodhounds refrain from tearing their victim to pieces when they have him at bay; but Larry stood there before his tormentors, young and ignorant and defenseless and offering to surrender, but they gave him no quarter.

He told them over and over that he wasn't trying to deny anything. He just didn't know why he did it. He tried saying "Yes" to whatever any of them suggested, but this didn't satisfy them either. They asked him if he thought he'd "get the chair." When he said he'd rather that than life imprisonment, they wanted to know why.

He looked around desperately to see if there wasn't someone to whom he could appeal for help. A large, red-faced woman, dressed in a police uniform, was on the other side of the room, talking to a girl who appeared to be drunk. Larry caught her eye. She came over to him at once and asked in a loud, coarse voice, "What goes on here?" One of the reporters pointed to Larry and said, "This kid is going to be charged with murder or attempted murder, maybe, and we're trying to get a story." Immediately she came back with, "You're wasting your time. Your papers can't print nothing about a juvenile, and you know it." Some of them were inclined to argue the point with her, saying, "Murder is murder, no matter who commits it," but most of them seemed to know her, and they laughingly told her to "go along with yourself, and tend to your knitting." When they saw that she was going to stand her ground, they agreed that they had about as much as they could get out of the boy, and they left for their papers to write up the sensational story for their public.

When they had gone, the policewoman told Larry that it was lucky for him that she had happened along because those devilish reporters were far worse than the District Attorney himself. She asked Larry if his mother knew he was in trouble, and when he answered, "No," she offered to phone her.

His mother wasn't home, and he looked at the clock and tried to think where his father would be at three in the afternoon. He was amazed to find that he couldn't remember what day of the week it was. He tried to think back. He had gone to get Mary on Friday morning, the day before Christmas Eve. That seemed such a long time ago. It couldn't be possible that it was still the Friday before Christmas. He asked the policewoman, and she said it was. He gave her the telephone number of his father's office and asked her to try to get his father. She came back beaming; she had talked to his father and he'd be right down.

While he was waiting, he thought of phoning Mary's mother to make sure that the hospital had notified her about Mary. Mr. Marty answered the phone, but Larry's voice was so hoarse that he didn't recognize it. Larry had to tell him who he was, and before he had a chance to say anything more, Mr. Marty asked, "Where's Mary?"

Evidently they hadn't been notified, and it was up to him to tell them. He didn't tell the whole truth, but even telling that Mary had been badly hurt was the hardest thing he had ever done in his life. He stammered and choked, and he finally made Mr. Marty understand that Mary was in the hospital. When Mr. Marty asked solicitously if he too had been hurt, he felt "like a dog." Then Mary's mother came to the telephone and asked the name of the hospital and wanted to know if Mary was "badly hurt," and Larry had to say, "Yes, badly."

He sat down on a bench and held his head between his hands. The policewoman came over and tried to comfort him. She said that it might not be so bad after all, that his father might be able to hire a good lawyer to get him out of his trouble. But he told her he wasn't worried about what was going to happen to him. The tears coursed down his cheeks as he thought of Mary's parents and the bitter sorrow in store for them.

He was thinking that Mary might be dead already, for all he knew, when his father came in. Larry told him the whole story, making no attempt to excuse himself or to explain why he had done it. His father said it was impossible. He couldn't believe it, but Larry told him he had to believe it because it was true. When his father said he'd get in touch with his lawyers immediately, Larry told him that wouldn't do any good. "If Mary dies, I'm going to take the punishment for killing her." He told his father the only thing he might be able to do was to get his doctors to see if anything could be done for Mary, if she was still alive.

Then Larry's mother came. She was in tears although she hadn't the slightest idea of what had happened. She had been told that he was being held by the police, and she knew he must be in trouble of some kind, though she didn't dream that it was anything more serious than violating the traffic laws. Larry's father looked at her pityingly. "You tell her, son. I can't." And so Larry had to go over the story once more. He had told it so often that now he recited it almost mechanically. His mother's first words showed that she found it even more difficult to believe than his father had. "Larry, I must be losing my mind. Surely, my boy can't be telling me that he deliberately strangled a girl without any reason." Larry repeated that he didn't know why he had done it and that there was no use to keep on asking why. He said he was very sorry, not only for Mary, but for her parents because he didn't know how they could get along without her if she died.

Through the weeks that followed, when Mary's death was momentarily awaited, Larry worried about her father and mother. It hadn't occurred to him that his own parents were suffering as much as Mary's, until his mother one day asked him, "What about us, Larry? Don't you think your father and I are as much to be pitied as Mary's parents?" But Larry was unmoved. "Oh, that's different. You're just worrying because you're afraid I'm going to be punished for something I did. But Mary never did anything, and her father and mother shouldn't have to suffer for something your son did."

The lawyers employed by Larry's father almost threw up their hands during these trying weeks. Larry could tell by their questions that they thought he was concealing something from them. They asked him over and over if he was sure Mary hadn't done anything to provoke his attack upon her. He said she hadn't. She had tried to get out of the car, but he certainly should have expected that, after the way he had frightened her almost to death. He went over the whole thing with them many times, trying not to leave out anything that had happened. When he said that Mary had pushed him away when he tried to kiss her, and the lawyers wanted to know if she had hurt him, he answered, "Of course not!"

They noticed that whenever he referred to Mary, he used the past tense, as though she were already dead. When they asked him about this, he said, "I hope she's not going to die. But even if she gets well, she's past tense for me. I could never go near her, because how do I know that the same thing wouldn't come over me again?"

When the lawyers told Larry's father that they didn't see what kind of defense they could make, since Larry admitted everything and absolved the girl from all blame, he demanded to know if they were just going to sit back and let his son go to the electric chair. They thought it was unlikely that a sixteen-year-old boy would be sentenced to the chair, but they weren't at all sure that he wouldn't get life imprisonment if Mary died.

Whenever anyone visited Larry, the only thing he wanted to know was, "How's Mary? Is she any better?" It was a long time before there was any word other than that the doctors had said she was no worse. When the glad tidings came that she had been pronounced out of danger the news was rushed to Larry. Even the District Attorney went in and shook hands with him and told him that the case was over as far as he was concerned.

But the case was just starting for us, although we did have some knowledge of it together with the reports of numerous psychiatrists, psychologists, and other experts who had examined Larry while he was in prison. We wanted some of the doctors to see Larry again because we thought the results might be different now that he was no longer confined and was relieved of the haunting fear of Mary's death. But the case continued to baffle them. Everything indicated that he had acted under the compulsion of an irresistible impulse, but as to the cause of the impulse and his inability to resist it, they could tell us nothing. Nor could they give us any assurance that there would never be a recurrence.

When Mary was strong enough to be interviewed, she told all that she knew about Larry. It was not much, for she had known him less than a year. A tear fell on her pillow, as she said, "I'm sorry I don't understand why he did it. If I did, I'd tell you. I'd like to help him in any way I could."

We had many conferences with Larry and his parents and more conferences with the lawyers and doctors and experts. It was finally agreed that our Court would commit Larry to what was considered the outstanding mental institution in the country. He will remain there as long as necessary for observation and treatment and will not be released unless and until the staff of the institution is able to assume the responsibility for his discharge. Larry understands that it may mean that he will have to spend the rest of his life in the institution, but he has been very brave. We feel that he is fortunate, even in his misfortune, because if his parents hadn't been able and willing to assume the almost prohibitive expense of this plan, the alternative would have offered little hope for "Lucky Larry."

8

PROSTITUTE'S DAUGHTER

The police officers who brought Kate and her child, Janie, into our Court were furious. They declared in strong language that it was the worst "contributing case" they had ever encountered; they hoped the mother would get "what was coming to her." By this they meant that they thought they had sufficient evidence of the neglect or mistreatment, or both, of this child by its mother, to warrant the maximum penalty provided by law. They proclaimed loudly, for the benefit of the District Attorney as well as the Court, "If this woman (pointing to Kate) don't get the limit, we may as well give up and go home and stay there."

We were fortunate in having assigned to our Court a District Attorney who understood that our primary purpose was saving the child, rather than punishing the parent. But the majority of the police force, though kind-hearted and well-meaning, had little respect for this point of view. Their sympathy for the child never extended to the parent; nor did they understand that the strong tie, which binds children to even the worst of parents, frequently makes it impossible to punish the parent without hurting the child. We had dwelt on this topic at great length whenever we were given the opportunity to discuss it with training classes at headquarters, but we could count few converts to our way of thinking. Most of the cops got boiling mad every time they found a neglected child, and they continued to vent their anger upon the parent whom they considered responsible for the child's condition, without considering the possibility that the parent herself might be the victim of "man's inhumanity to man."

Long familiarity with their attitude made us allow for exaggeration in a case such as the one before us. But we found later that there had been no need for exaggeration, for even the emotional police officers could conjure up nothing worse than the conditions under which Kate and her child had been living.

Their abode had long been in the rear part of what had once been an old feed store on the fringe of the Vieux Carre. There were no sanitary conveniences of any kind because the premises had never been used for residential purposes until Kate had moved into them. There was one large room with a bed and a cubbyhole just big enough for Janie's cot and an oil cooking stove. The roof leaked "like a basket," and the floors and sills were so rotten that they would support little weight except in the few spots where Kate had placed her "furniture." The entire place was overrun with vermin, and rats "as big as dogs" could be heard day and night "playing fate" in the walls and attic.

It was easy enough to believe this as we looked at Kate. Her clothing was dirty and disheveled, and her

hair was so matted that it would have been impossible to
draw a comb through it. The deep lines in her face were
encrusted with dirt which had become embedded in the
skin. But what concerned us most was the look of abject
despair which pervaded her whole person.

Many of the women of her calling came into Court
defiant and ready to fight "for their rights," but Kate stood
there dejectedly and let the officers say what they would
about her. It was only when they mentioned Janie that
terror seemed to creep over her, and she looked at the
Court appealingly. We wanted to say something that
would make her feel a little better, and yet we did not
wish to mislead her by reassuring remarks for which we
saw no basis at this stage of the proceedings. We had
noticed that, in contrast to the mother's unkempt appearance, Janie looked very clean and neat in her nicely laundered cotton dress. And so, as we groped in our mind for
words to allay some of the fear in the mother's eyes, we
smiled at Janie and asked, "Who laundered your dress so
beautifully?" The child looked at her mother for answer; and though neither of them spoke, we could feel
that there was a little less tension after that.

We usually had to discourage the officers from dwelling
too much on "physical conditions," but there were elements in this case which the officers themselves recognized as more important than the particulars about "the
dilapidated old building" in which Kate and her child
had been living. According to their report, Kate was a
prostitute of the lowest class, and they could produce
evidence to prove that "she took anything that came
along, including drunks, hopheads, and chinamen."

We listened to everything they had to say, and then
we heard the whole story from Kate. If it had not been

for the child, there probably would have been little to distinguish Kate's life from that of the thousands of other women who practice "the oldest profession in the world" in the large cities of our country.

She had come to our city at the age of eighteen to escape the drudgery of her uncle's farm, which had been her lot ever since her parents' death. She had always had enough to eat and a place to sleep, and she was disappointed to find that, even in the city, she had to work hard to earn enough for food and lodging. She had tried one job after another, when she met some girls from a call house who invited her to join them. From what they told her, it looked like an easy way to get money for the pretty clothes and other nice things she had dreamed of, but she never intended to "stay in the game" after she had accomplished her purpose.

When Kate first went to live in "the house," there were a number of girls there who were even younger than she was, and she thought that all of them were much prettier than she, but the madam of the house was soon getting requests to "send Kate," instead of the usual "send a girl and be sure she's young and pretty." The other girls didn't like this, because they were supposed to be sent out in rotation and the madam paid them ten dollars a call. Kate protested that she never asked any of the taxi drivers, bartenders, or other procurers to call for her, but the girls didn't believe it; and when several of the youngest and prettiest left to go to another house, the madam told Kate that she would have to find another place.

Not knowing where to go, Kate asked the madam, and at her suggestion she went to a house which turned out to be entirely different from the call house. The men who came to this house weren't the same type as those she served when she went out on "calls," and the girls were all much older than Kate. She was sure that some of them were old enough to be her grandmother. The madam was a big woman with a coarse voice, who treated the girls more like animals than human beings; but once again Kate found herself popular with the customers, and she seldom got more than two hours of continuous sleep either day or night. The madam bought all the clothes, and Kate was allowed to go out so seldom that she felt almost like a prisoner.

She was miserable and unhappy, and she tried to think of a way out of her desperate situation. She knew the names of a few of the taxi drivers who seemed to like her, and she called them and asked for help. They said they were sorry for her, but they couldn't afford to get her madam "sore" at them because she knew enough about them to send them to jail. It was the same with the police officers, who would have liked to help. The madam had "too much on them." When she told some of the older women in the house about her efforts, they laughed at her and asked, "Don't you know that the madam splits with the taxi drivers on everything they bring her and that she pays the police for protection?" They told her that her only hope was to get one of the customers interested in her. They had all sorts of ideas about how to accomplish this, and Kate was trying some of them out when she got "hooked."

She went on working because she didn't dare tell the madam. But the girls were sympathetic, and when she was within three months of her time, they went to the madam in a group and told her she'd have to give "the kid" a rest until she was over her trouble. The next three months seemed more like years as Kate waited impatiently for what she hoped would be her deliverance from the bondage of the life she had chosen. The madam would have to let her go to the hospital, and when her trouble was over, she'd never return to that house. But when her time finally came, she didn't even know it. One of the girls found her lying unconscious on the floor of the bathroom, and she knew nothing until she opened her eyes several days later in the hospital and heard a nurse saying, "Well, you almost didn't make it. But you're going to be all right now. And you have a beautiful little girl. Want to see her?"

She had known that she was going to have a baby, but what she didn't know was that the baby would be a person. She found that out now, when the nurse put Janie in her arms. The child looked at her out of round blue eyes and then snuggled into her breast. Then Kate realized that this wasn't just another baby, it was her child and it already knew her and loved her. Her heart overflowed with joy, and she reveled in her new-found happiness, until one of the girls from the house came to see her and asked her what she was going to do with the baby.

It had never occurred to Kate during the long days of waiting that she would want to keep her baby when it came, but now she knew she couldn't part with it.

When she was discharged from the hospital, she went back to "the house" because she had no other place to go. She was proudly showing the baby to "madam's girls" when madam herself came in, and without even glancing at the baby, asked coldly, "What are you going to do with it?" Kate was almost too frightened to answer, but she looked down at the baby and tried to be brave. "I'm going to keep it."

"Impossible!" yelled madam, glaring at the baby as though it were some monster. The girls tried to soften the blow by explaining to Kate that the police couldn't let madam operate with a baby in the house. Madam made it even clearer by adding, "No matter how much I paid them, they couldn't let me do it. They'd be kicked off the force, and then where would we be?"

Kate made a few half-hearted attempts to place the baby in an orphan asylum, but she was ashamed to answer some of the questions they asked her. She didn't know who Janie's father was, and she didn't know what they would think if she told them it could have been any one of a large number of men, most of whose names were unknown to her.

They told her that they might be willing to keep the baby for a year, if she would agree to surrender it for adoption in case she couldn't provide a proper home for it by the end of that time. When she heard this, she thanked them and said she'd keep it.

And so she did, through ten long years. She supported it in the only way she could, hoping always to find some other way before the child was old enough to understand.

She couldn't stay in any "house" because of the baby, and she found it very hard to make out on her own. The madams could use political influence, when the cost of police protection became prohibitive, and the call girls had friends who could help them out when they got in a jam. But Kate, without either friends or influence, had to pay whatever was demanded.

When Janie was a tiny baby, she made a little cradle for her from one of the bureau drawers, which she could shove under the bed when anyone came into her room. In this way she managed to keep her existence a secret for some time. But the child soon grew too big for this, and it was then that she moved to the old building in which she had been found by the police. It was dark and dingy, and her only entrance was through a narrow alley. But it had the advantage of the small cubicle of a room, which she called the kitchen and in which she could put a cot for Janie. She always kept the door of her room tightly closed when she had anyone with her, but Janie woke up one night, and before Kate knew it, she had pushed the door open and had come into the room. When Kate saw her, she was pointing to a half-dressed man standing beside her mother's bed and asking, "Who's that?"

The man said, "My God!" and rushed out. He must have reported it to the police, because the officer on the beat came to see Kate the next day and asked about the child. Kate pleaded with him to give her a chance to find a place for the child, and when she saw that he was going to refuse, she went to the bed and took a wallet containing fifty dollars from under the mattress. It had been dropped by one of her "customers," and she knew he would come back to claim it, but she took the money out and gave it to the cop. He took it without promising anything, and the new cop who took his place a few days later said nothing about the child, but he demanded twice as much money as she had paid the other man.

There was only one way in which she could raise the sums now being required of her, and she was very reluctant to resort to it. She knew that, although most prostitutes were honest, many of them were wrongfully accused of stealing from their patrons; and she despised the few dishonest ones, who made things so hard for all the others. But she lived in constant fear and dread of being arrested; she didn't know what might happen to the child if it were left alone. She told herself that her prices were much lower than those charged by the madams, and she began slipping a few dollars from the pockets of unsuspecting customers. She was always careful not to take all they had, and if any of them came back, looking for the money they had lost, she promptly found it and gave it back to them. She was sure that most of them never missed what she took, and in this way she managed for several years.

When Kate moved to the feed store, she had thought it an advantage that there would be no neighbors to bother her about the child. But one evening the police picked her up for streetwalking and held her in jail overnight. She almost lost her mind worrying about the child being alone in "that dump," picturing Janie frightened and crying her heart out. She prayed that someone would go to the child. Janie, though, was all right when her mother got home the next morning; but Kate couldn't get it off her mind until she let a guy buy her a drink. It made her feel good, and after that she got the habit of taking a drink whenever things got too tough. She didn't eat or sleep regularly, and before long she was depending upon drink to take the place of both food and rest.

She had long since lost all the freshness of youth, and now that she made no attempt to keep herself clean or neat, she began to look like a haggard old woman. When she accosted men on the streets, they chased her away with a curse. Drunks and "hopheads" and others who had sunk to the lowest depths of human depravity were now her only customers, and "Kate's Alley" became notorious for fights and brawls and disgraceful goings-on.

Through it all, she sent Janie to school "in a clean, ironed dress" every day. She held her head up as she said this, and Janie smiled proudly.

She had admitted even more than the cops had said about her, but we asked her if she would like the Court to appoint an attorney to represent her. She shook her head sadly, and not being sure that she understood what we meant, we explained her legal rights. But she shook her head again and said, "It's no use. The cops are right. I'm not fit to have her."

Janie began to cry at this, and Kate's tears began to flow too, but we knew from her next words that they were tears of resignation, not of rebellion. She looked at her child, and all the love that was in her heart shone out through her eyes as she said, "You know what you have to do, and you'll do it. I should have done it myself, only I couldn't. But there's just one favor I'd like to ask. You thought her dress was done up nice. Could you fix it so I would be able to wash and iron her clothes for her? She likes the way I do them, and it might make her feel that I'm not so very far away."

Only a love like Kate's could have inspired such a perfect plan to make it easier for Janie to bear the separation from her mother. During the years that followed, it was often the only bright spot in a very dark picture. The way back to decency was a long, hard road for Kate, and we knew she was often on the verge of giving up, but she never failed to have Janie's laundry ready on time. It might seem a very insignificant thing to some people, but we knew that Kate hadn't entirely lost faith in herself as long as she continued to bring in those exquisitely laundered garments.

We didn't always see Kate when she came in, but we were aware that the probation officer sometimes had to decide that she was in no condition to visit Janie. She chose to regard this as her "punishment," although we tried to convince her that our only purpose was to avoid embarrassing Janie in the foster home in which she had been getting along so nicely.

We attempted no explanation to Janie when her mother couldn't visit her, but we always tried to break the news to her when a big box of her mother's laundry was being delivered to her. We knew that the work of Kate's loving hands could speak to her child more eloquently than any words of ours.

When Janie was sixteen, she asked for permission to leave school and get a job. We conferred with her teachers and the school counselors, and it was agreed that Janie's concern for her mother was making it so hard for her to concentrate on her studies that it might be advisable to let her have her wish. We told Janie that we hoped she would complete her education at some time in the future, but we found a place for her with a fashionable dressmaker.

Janie was enthusiastic about her work from the very beginning. She learned to sew very quickly, and when she came in to see us in some of the lovely dresses she designed and made for herself, she looked like a beautiful picture. She worked very hard, and before the end of the year she was transferred to the cutting and fitting department of the shop. This meant a substantial increase in salary, and Janie could hardly wait to tell us about it and ask, "Is it enough?" We knew that she meant, Was it enough for her to set up housekeeping and take her mother to live with her?

When we hesitated about approving the plan, because we didn't want to see Janie hurt, she got out a notebook and showed us that she had it figured out to a penny. Seeing that we were still doubtful, she answered what was in our minds. "Don't worry about mother. She'll be all right now, but even if she isn't, I can take care of her. She started drinking because she was so worried about me. And when you took me away from her, she couldn't stop, because she never really believed that she would ever get me back again. You'll see how different it will be with her, if you'll just let me try to help her."

When we announced the plan to Kate, we were careful not to let her see any of the doubts that were lurking in our minds, and we were therefore much surprised when we found that she shared them. "You know I wouldn't want to disgrace her, but I lose hold of myself sometimes, and I don't seem to be able to help it." When she saw that nothing that she could say would shatter Janie's faith in her, she consented to "visit" Janie for a while, to see "how it worked out."

It worked very well, for Kate was kept so busy cleaning and scouring everything in the apartment, and cooking and washing for Janie, that she was seldom tempted to lapse back into her old ways. The intervals between back-slidings became longer and longer, until finally there were no further recurrences.

We sometimes think that of all the young people we know Janie is the happiest. She is studying drawing and designing at night school and has shown so much aptitude and talent that we wouldn't be surprised to see her become one of the top fashion designers of the country. She loves to bring her friends home and have them admire her mother in the becoming creations which she fashions for her and which Kate wears so well and so proudly.

And the more we hear of all this, the more are we filled with wonder. During the formative years of her life, Janie was surrounded by every influence calculated to produce delinquency. Yet, she came through it all unscathed. If we knew why, we would know a great deal more about the prediction and treatment of delinquency than has as yet been discovered. We can venture a guess, though there is no way of proving whether we are right or wrong. But if we had to put our finger on one thing which we think saved Janie, it would be the strength of her mother's love for her and of her love for her mother. For those who would ask about other mothers, whose children became delinquents, in spite of love which was apparently as great as Kate's, we have no answer, except another question: "How do you measure love?"

9

HANDSOME BOY

The lights at the entrance to the Juvenile Court were hardly visible in the gray fog of the morning, but for Mrs. Norton, standing under them, they were rays of hope which helped her wait for the big doors to open.

A few minutes before seven the custodian arrived with a bunch of keys and looked inquiringly at Mrs. Norton. She answered his unspoken question with, "Can I see the Judge?"

Although not unaccustomed to early callers, the custodian didn't feel obliged to adhere too strictly to Court rules about "being courteous to everyone" at this hour of the morning. He replied rather brusquely. "Yes, you can see her when she gets here. But she don't sleep here."

Mrs. Norton knew he thought she was too early, but she was too worried to care greatly about anything except seeing the Judge at the earliest possible moment. She followed the custodian up the double flight of stairs. When they reached the top, he motioned her into the courtroom and then went in the opposite direction.

She was still standing there when he came back, loaded down with buckets and mops. He went to work at his cleaning job without even glancing in her direction. She could see that he didn't want to be bothered, but she couldn't refrain from going over to him every now and then with a question. "Will I be the first one to see the Judge?" "How will I know when she gets here?" "Do you have to have an appointment?" "Will you tell her I've been waiting since six o'clock?" Finally he turned on her in exasperation. "If you don't let me alone, Madame, the people will start piling in here before I get this half-done."

He must have been sorry that he hadn't been a little nicer to her, when she said humbly, "Please excuse me, I'm so nervous." He stopped his work once more and explained. "Yes, M'am. I can see you are. But all of them that comes here are upset about something. The Judge says that most of them have been worrying all night, and we shouldn't mind it if they act nervous. I'm sorry if I was a little short with you. But don't you worry, the Judge will be along directly, and she'll see you right away."

She felt better after this and sat down and waited quietly until she saw someone pass through the courtroom and go into a small office at the left of the rostrum. She looked around for the custodian, but he had disappeared. She walked quickly over to the office door, and seeing that it was open, she went in and smilingly exclaimed, "You're the Judge! I'd know you anywhere from your pictures!" But the light faded from her eyes as she added, "But I never thought I'd be coming to see you about my boy."

Mrs. Norton reached into her purse and brought out a photograph of a strikingly handsome boy, which she placed on the desk with the words, "This is Stanley. He's fifteen now, but he was only twelve when this was taken. Everybody has always said he was too pretty to be a boy." Her eyes filled with tears, and knowing that it would do her good to cry a little, we looked at the picture again and said nothing for the next few minutes. When we thought she might be able to regain her composure, we asked, "Does he still look as much like you now, or has he changed since he started to grow up?" At this her face lighted up with pleasure. "Oh, you think he looks like me? Well, maybe a little, but he's so much better looking than I ever was."

We handed the picture back to her. She held it lovingly against her heart as she told us why she had come to the Court for help. We asked her to tell us everything she could remember about the boy, and we could see that she was trying very hard not to omit anything that might be important.

His father had died when Stanley was four years old, and she had worked to support him ever since. Her mother-in-law, who had lived with her for several years after her husband's death, had been a great help in caring for the boy. She was devoted to Stanley, "the only child of her only child," and he was all that she lived for. Nevertheless, she was a little jealous of Stanley's mother; in spite of all she did for the boy, she thought he loved his mother more than he did her.

Mrs. Norton explained that this was probably due to the fact that she was away all day; he was naturally glad to see her and wanted to be with her every minute after she came home. She wished his grandmother could have known how he missed her after she died. He was eleven years old at the time; he "took it very hard" and grieved so much that his mother was worried about him.

She often found him moping in the kitchen when she
came home from work, instead of playing outside with
the neighborhood children. She "got after him" about it,
but it didn't seem to do any good.

She was "really glad" when he made friends with
Mr. Brooks. She knew the boy was lonely, and Mr.
Brooks was such a "nice" man. She wasn't surprised that
he had "taken a fancy" to Stanley; grown people had always liked the boy. He was polite and serious, and his
teachers said he was a "little gentleman." Mrs. Norton
thought his grandmother was entitled to all the credit for
that because "she raised him in the old-fashioned way
and taught him to have respect for his elders, no matter
who they were."

Although Mrs. Norton's salary was barely enough to
pay the rent and buy food and a few clothes, she managed to give Stanley a small allowance. He never com-
plained about the amount she gave him, but she realized
that it was less than other boys of his age received from
their parents. She also knew that most boys in his school
had more of everything than Stanley did. This worried
her, but there was nothing she could do about it because
it seemed that the harder she worked and the more she
earned, the more expensive everything became. She
didn't like to buy things on the "never, never plan," but
she had made up her mind that it was the only way she
would be able to get Stanley the bicycle he needed when
he started junior high school. She thought that the new
school was too far for Stanley to walk, and the bicycle
would be cheaper than bus fare. Besides, he had been
wanting a bicycle for a long time.

But before she "got around to it," Mr. Brooks had
bought Stanley a beautiful bicycle "loaded" with acces-

sories of all kinds. Mrs. Norton was even more delighted than the boy, and she told Mr. Brooks that he was "a real fairy godfather."

That was only the beginning. There seemed to be no end to what Mr. Brooks was willing to do for the boy. He bought him a rod and reel and a skiff and took him out fishing every week end during the summer. When winter came, he bought him a gun and taught him to shoot, and Stanley became wild about hunting. Mrs. Norton was very happy to see the boy getting all the things she couldn't afford to give him, and she made no objection when he started spending every week end with Mr. Brooks, though she did miss him terribly.

She didn't know anybody who knew Mr. Brooks, and when she asked him what he did for a living, he said that he was "in business." He was always so nice to her that when she saw he didn't want to tell her anything more, she didn't press him. But she was concerned about the way he spent money so freely; she asked her office manager to get a report on him. When the report came back, she felt a little ashamed; it showed that Mr. Brooks was an important executive in a large corporation and that he "enjoyed a very high credit rating and an excellent reputation in the community."

This satisfied her. She had few misgivings after that. Mr. Brooks bought expensive clothes for Stanley and was very proud of how handsome he looked in them. He disarmed her completely by buying fine presents for the boy to give her. How could she be so ungrateful as to refuse to let Stanley go out with Mr. Brooks and keep him company whenever he asked?

Mr. Brooks had succeeded in convincing her of his great loneliness by telling her how he had worshiped his mother and how he didn't think life would ever again be worth living after she died. Mrs. Norton was much impressed when he invited her to his home and showed her photographs of his mother on the walls of many rooms in the house, as well as a life-size oil painting, which he had had made after her death. Once again Mrs. Norton chided herself for ever having thought of doubting a man who had been so devoted to his mother.

Mr. Brooks always seemed to have Stanley's interest at heart. When the boy wanted a motorcycle, he said, "That's too dangerous. You might be killed or crippled for life." He made up for it by buying Stanley a horse that he could ride when they went to the country.

Stanley had done very well at school while his grandmother was alive, but after her death he had no one to help him with his homework. His mother didn't get home until six in the evening, and she then had to cook dinner, clean the house, and get her clothes and his ready for the next day. Stanley was usually fast asleep by the time she had finished her chores.

After he started going out with Mr. Brooks, he fell even further behind in his studies. Several bad reports in succession made his mother decide that he had too many distractions and that he'd have to stay home and study on school nights. Stanley hadn't mentioned anything to Mr. Brooks about the poor grades he was making in school until he told him about his mother's decision. Mr. Brooks asked to see the reports. He was sure Stanley wouldn't be promoted unless he was coached, and he employed one of the best teachers in the school to help Stanley. The boy's grades improved rapidly. This, of course, pleased his mother, although she didn't like to ask the coach to come to her place to teach Stanley, since he was being paid by Mr. Brooks. Nor did she want to spoil the boy's pleasure by asking him to stay home with her once in a while on a week end or a holiday.

She told herself that she should be glad that Stanley had a fine man like Mr. Brooks to take the place of his father; otherwise he might have become a sissy from being tied first to his grandmother's apron strings and then to hers.

Some of her friends asked questions about Mr. Brooks which indicated that they didn't altogether approve of him. She showed them the report about his financial standing and his fine reputation, and she told them about his devotion to his mother. When they still seemed skeptical, she attributed it to the fact that they were peeved because he paid no attention to them. She wanted them to like him, and she knew they would if they were acquainted with him. She couldn't think of any way to bring this about until she met an attractive young lady who was visiting one of her friends, and she had the "bright idea" of giving a party for the visitor the following Sunday and inviting Mr. Brooks.

She made all the arrangements and waited for Mr. Brooks to drop in, so that she could tell him about the party. When he finally came on Friday, she had the house all "dolled up," and she asked him if he could guess "what for?" He couldn't. When she told him, she was very disappointed that he wouldn't be able to come. She tried to persuade him that if he was just going to take Stanley some place, he could call it off because she thought Stanley was getting a little fed-up with those week-end trips anyway. When she said this, Mr. Brooks looked as though she had stabbed him, and she almost thought he was going to cry as he said, "You mean he doesn't like me any more?" He seemed to be so distressed that Mrs. Norton tried "to pass it off as a joke." She said she was only trying to get Mr. Brooks to come to her party so that she could "make a match for him."

He didn't come to the party, but he told Stanley what she had said about him, and when the boy came home, he asked his mother how she knew. "Knew what?" she asked. "How did you know I'm getting fed up with always going out just with Mr. Brooks and nobody else?" She had to confess that she hadn't thought of it, that it had just come out on the spur of the moment when she was trying to persuade Mr. Brooks to call off the week end trip.

Stanley said it was true; he had tried to tell Mr. Brooks several times that he appreciated all he had done for him, but he would like to go out with some kids his own age sometimes. But Mr. Brooks always got so hurt and said he knew Stanley didn't like him and that he didn't blame him because nobody liked him. Then Stanley would have to tell him how much he did like him and that he hadn't meant what he said about wanting to be with the boys.

Mrs. Norton had noticed that although Mr. Brooks went out of his way to find out about things that Stanley would like to have, he would never consent to his bringing other boys along when they went for an outing. She thought Stanley wanted this because it was the one thing Mr. Brooks wouldn't permit. She tried to explain this to Mr. Brooks the next time she saw him. She said that since Mr. Brooks had been providing Stanley with clothes and spending money, she had been able to save a few dollars, and she asked Mr. Brooks if he didn't think it would be a good idea to satisfy Stanley's desire to be with young people his own age by letting him go to camp during vacation. When Mr. Brooks construed this as meaning that she thought that Stanley hated him and wanted to get away from him, she gave up and said no more about it.

He took Stanley for a wonderful trip through the Canadian Rockies that summer, and although the boy was too young to get a driver's license, he taught him to drive and let him take the wheel whenever they were out on the open road. When Stanley told his mother about driving, she was worried. She was even more worried when he told her that Mr. Brooks had promised him a plane trip for his fifteenth birthday. Mrs. Norton was "deathly afraid" of planes, and Mr. Brooks knew it, and she thought he was going a little too far in his efforts to please Stanley.

On the day before they were to leave, she bought a birthday cake and gave Stanley his birthday presents, saying, "You won't be here on your birthday, son, but I'd like you to stay home with me tonight." Stanley stayed, and they talked about everything under the sun— except neither of them mentioned Mr. Brooks. Mrs. Norton didn't want Stanley to know that she was a little sore at Mr. Brooks about the airplane trip. She guessed that Stanley must have had some reason of his own for not referring to his friend.

Stanley seemed to be very sleepy when he went to bed, but his mother could hear him moving about in his room a long time afterward. She couldn't imagine what he was doing, because he was all packed for the trip. Thinking that he might be ill, she got up and went to his room and found him sitting on the side of his bed with his head in his hands. She sat down beside him and asked him what was the matter. He got up and walked to the window and looked out before he answered. "I was going to wait until morning, but I suppose I might as well ask you now and get it over with." "Ask me what Stanley? You know you don't have to be afraid to ask me anything." Then the boy buried his head in his mother's shoulder and cried as though his heart would break.

She didn't know how long it was, but it must have been nearly an hour before he finally managed to sob out, "Mother, can I go to live with Mr. Brooks?" She felt his head to see if he had a fever before she said, "What are you talking about, Stanley? You know you don't want to leave your mother and go to live with Mr. Brooks or anybody else." Then he blurted out, "I know I don't want to, Mother, but I have to. I'm in so deep already that I can't get out. He'll kill me if I try." And then she knew. It came to her suddenly, and she cried out in agony, "Oh, you poor boy. You have a foolish, stupid mother. How could I have been so blind? But why didn't you tell me before?"

He pushed her away from him and stood up trembling with fear, as he cried, "Mother, I haven't told you anything. But he'll think I did, and he'll kill me. He said he would, Mother, if I ever told anybody."

Now Mrs. Norton saw clearly the meaning of many things that had occurred during the past three years. It was all so plain that it was impossible to understand how she hadn't seen it before. She remembered all the hints her friends had tried to give her. They must have suspected Mr. Brooks all along, but they knew she didn't, and they had been afraid to come right out and say anything. If only they had, before things had gone so far that her boy's life was in danger.

The little that she knew about homosexuals had been gleaned from sensational newspaper accounts of the brutal crimes committed by them. She had always thought that they belonged to the lowest stratum of humanity, and she would never have dreamed of suspecting a man of Mr. Brooks' education and refinement of such depravity. She was sure that he must be insane; that was the only way she could reconcile what he had done with what she knew him to be.

She checked all the doors and windows to make certain they were locked, and then she sat by Stanley's bed for the rest of the night. He slept fitfully, and she hated to awaken him when it was time for her to leave. But she had to get him up so that he could come to the door with her and bolt it from the inside when she went out. She did not go down the steps until she heard him draw the latch.

When she had completed her story, we told her we thought it was a case for the District Attorney, and we sent for him. After we outlined the facts for him very briefly, he asked Mrs. Norton if the boy would testify against Mr. Brooks. She said she thought he would be afraid to do that, and besides he was very fond of Mr. Brooks and appreciated all that he had done for him. She admitted that, as a matter of fact, the boy hadn't actually told her anything. We explained to her that, while her suspicions were probably well founded, you couldn't prosecute a man on mere suspicion of indecent behavior with a juvenile. We told her that in any event we would have to talk to the boy.

She tried to telephone him, and when she received no answer, she became so panic-stricken that we offered to let one of our officers go with her to try to find him. They

went first to her home and then to the house of Mr.
Brooks. When they arrived at the door, they heard what
sounded like fighting and scuffling going on inside and
then the voice of a boy screaming, "Let me go, I tell
you. Let me go." Mrs. Norton recognized the voice as
Stanley's, and she became hysterical. She wanted the
officer to break down the door, but instead he rang the
bell.

Mr. Brooks opened the door, and when he saw Stanley's mother, he asked her to come in. The house was
in disorder, with tables and chairs overturned and furnishings strewn over the floor. Stanley's clothes were rent and
torn as were Mr. Brooks', and both boy and man looked
as though they had been through a fierce struggle. Mr.
Brooks was the first to speak. "I don't know what's the
matter with the kid. You can see for yourself that he's
hysterical, and I hope you won't believe a word of what
he's told you." Stanley looked at him defiantly. "I told
you that I hadn't told anything to anybody. But you
wouldn't believe me. And so now I'm going to tell everything."

They brought both Mr. Brooks and Stanley to the
Court, and the boy told us the whole ugly story of his
seduction.

He had first met the man at a magazine stand, where
he was looking at some comic books. Mr. Brooks asked
him which of the books he liked and then paid for the
ones Stanley picked out and gave them to him. When
Stanley thanked him, he said, "What are you waiting for?
You've got your books, let's go." They walked along together for a few blocks, and Mr. Brooks asked Stanley
how old he was and what school he attended and who
his parents were, before he said, "You're a nice kid and

I'd like to see you again some time. Tomorrow's Saturday, how about taking in a show?"

Stanley met him the following afternoon, and he said he hadn't eaten, and would Stanley mind going to dinner with him before the show? He let the boy order anything he wanted to eat, and when they had finished, he let him pick the show. The same thing happened the next Saturday, and after the show Mr. Brooks said he had something at his house he'd like to show Stanley. The boy went with him and found that it was a very interesting collection of old guns. Mr. Brooks explained how each one worked, and the boy was so fascinated that he forgot all about the lateness of the hour. Mr. Brooks drove him home, but his mother had been "worried to death" about him. He told her about his new friend, and she asked him how old he was. He didn't know then, but he found out later that Mr. Brooks was forty.

After that, he saw Mr. Brooks frequently, and he liked him "a lot." He knew Mr. Brooks thought he liked him only on account of all the presents he bought him, but it wasn't true. He really liked him for himself and because he talked to him just as if he were a grown-up man. In telling about it, Stanley explained, "I was just a little kid then, only twelve years old, and I thought it was fine to be 'bumming around' with a man like Mr. Brooks."

Stanley didn't remember how long this went on before Mr. Brooks "tried anything," but he knew it was a good while. Mr. Brooks bought him two complete outfits, "shoes and all," because he said he wanted Stanley to look nice when he went out with him. Stanley found that he could get almost anything he wanted by just mentioning it to Mr. Brooks, and he tried to show his appreciation by doing anything Mr. Brooks wanted. But he didn't like it when he started putting his hands on him. He wanted to stop him, but he didn't want to hurt his feelings, and so he let him go on. When he went too far, Stanley told him it was "nasty," but Mr. Brooks got so upset about it that Stanley told him he didn't mean it.

That's the way it went on. Whenever the boy objected to his advances, he'd say he didn't like him, and he'd "take on" so that Stanley always ended up by letting him do as he wanted. After a while he "got used to it," and he wouldn't have minded it much if Mr. Brooks hadn't always been warning him about what would happen if anybody found out. This made Stanley feel that what they were doing must be terribly wrong, and he wished there were somebody he could talk to about it.

But he never really started to worry about it too much until one day he heard the boys talking in the locker room at school. He overheard only part of what they said, but it was enough for him to suspect that they were talking about him. As soon as they saw him, they shut up, and he pretended to go off. But he sneaked back in through another door and listened again. This time there could be no mistake because they referred to him by name, and he heard one of them say, "He'll go nuts. They all do, if they keep it up."

He thought they were right, because he already felt as though he was going crazy. He didn't know what to do. Mr. Brooks had told him that he would go to jail, and Stanley would be put in a reform school if anybody found out. He didn't want Mr. Brooks to go to jail, and he had heard a lot of bad things about reform schools. But when he thought of being locked up in an insane asylum for the rest of his life, he decided that anything would be better than that.

Mr. Brooks was very angry when he told him that he couldn't go on because he was afraid that he was losing his mind. He accused Stanley of having talked to somebody, and when Stanley convinced him that he hadn't, he laughed at the idea of insanity and said it was nothing but "propaganda gotten out for the benefit of school boys."

Stanley continued to make attempts to break off with Mr. Brooks until the man finally told him that he would kill him if he tried it. After that Stanley lived in constant fear and dread of his former friend. When he spent the night with Mr. Brooks, he tried to stay awake because he was afraid that Mr. Brooks might kill him in his sleep. He no longer took any pleasure in any of the handsome things Mr. Brooks did for him, and he again began to ask if he couldn't take some of his friends along when they went for outings. He tried in every way he could to avoid being alone with Mr. Brooks, but it was to no avail. He succeeded only in wounding the man's pride and in making him more determined than ever not to let the boy "jilt" him.

As the time for his fifteenth birthday and the promised plane trip approached, Stanley told Mr. Brooks that his mother didn't want him to go. Mr. Brooks knew very well that Stanley had been very eager to make the trip in spite of his mother's fear of planes. He felt that the boy was actually beginning to hate him if he would forego the plane trip to avoid being with him.

He waited until the day before Stanley's birthday to tell him to ask his mother if he could come to live with him permanently. Stanley said it was no use to ask her; she wouldn't let him. But when Mr. Brooks hinted that there were ways of forcing her if she refused, Stanley not only agreed to ask her, but to try to make her believe it was what he wanted.

He intended to do just that, but he couldn't help crying when the time came to tell his mother that he wanted to leave her. And he couldn't help it when his mother guessed what had happened. He went to tell Mr. Brooks that his mother knew, but that he hadn't told her. He never would have testified against Mr. Brooks if he hadn't refused to believe him.

Having heard the rest of the story from Stanley's mother, we turned the case over to the District Attorney, insofar as Mr. Brooks was concerned. He employed the best legal talent available to defend his case, but he was found guilty of "indecent behavior with a juvenile" and given the maximum penalty provided by law for this offense. This was all that could be done for him under existing laws, but we realize that it does not solve his problem and that he will probably be more of a menace to society after he comes out of prison than he was when he went in.

Stanley was sent to the Guidance Center and the Clinic for examination and such treatment as was indicated. When we learned that he had emerged from his unfortunate experience without any permanent damage to his mind or body or spirit, we offered up a silent prayer of gratitude for the resiliency of youth.

10

ORPHANS OF DIVORCE

Sadie and Mae were as sullen and resentful a pair of young people as we had ever seen brought into the Court by detectives. According to the complaint before us, both girls were "under seventeen," but a heavy mask of make-up concealed their youthful complexions, and an over-liberal application of lipstick distorted their mouths into what was almost a grimace. Their eyebrows were plucked to a thin, artificial line, and their blouses were cut low enough to reveal indecently "uplifted" bosoms. Everything about them, from the waves of their carefully set hair to the extravagantly high heels of their shoes, bespoke great pains on their part to make themselves attractive to the opposite sex.

As we looked at them, we thought what a pity it was to cover up and pervert the freshness and charm of youth; and yet we realized that these girls, who had been picked up as "B-Drinkers," didn't look too different from the teen-age daughters of some of our friends.

The birth certificates which they had furnished the owner of the night spot, when he had hired them a few months previously, had shown ages above eighteen for both girls; but they now had to admit that they had "borrowed" these certificates from the daughters of the woman with whom they roomed. They had also assumed the names of the girls to whom the certificates belonged, but this seemed unimportant to them because they had been traveling around the country for some time under various aliases.

We soon found that they had no desire to cooperate with us. On the contrary, they did everything they could to keep us from finding out who they were. They offered to "take their medicine, whatever it was" and said we could "give them the works," but they would never tell us the names of their parents.

When the Bureau of Missing Persons was unable to identify the girls as any of those reported missing from their homes at the time, we asked them to go back further in their files and check the unsolved cases. This produced the description of two girls who had run away from a boarding school in a distant state, more than six months previously. It was a routine inquiry, which had probably been sent to every large city in the country, and it was quite possible that our Bureau would not have been notified, even though the girls had been found.

But it was our one clue, and we followed it up immediately by writing to the boarding school. It was some time before we received a reply to the effect that the officials of the boarding school didn't know whether or not their girls had been located. They had turned the matter over to the girls' parents and had no special interest in it as they never took girls back after they had run away.

We pursued the matter further by asking for the name and address of the parents of their girls; but we experienced another long delay because the boarding school felt that they could not give us this information without first obtaining the consent of the girls' parents.

It had been necessary for our girls to say they were sisters, in order to use the borrowed birth certificates. But even after it was discovered that the certificates were not theirs, they continued to say they were sisters. We thought they looked alike, even when they came in without the make-up which had given them the appearance of identical twins. It therefore looked as though we had been on the wrong trail, when the boarding school finally gave us the names and addresses of two different sets of parents. We wired the parents and received prompt replies from them stating that their daughters had not been found and asking us to give descriptions of the girls we were holding.

We sent for Sadie and Mae and showed them the telegrams. They quickly explained the two sets of parents. The telegram signed "Ada and William Abbott" was from their father and stepmother. The one signed "Elizabeth and Robert Benton" was from their mother and stepfather. The girls were indeed sisters and "almost twins," being separated in age by only thirteen months. Mae attempted to explain. "For one whole month every year it seems like Sadie is two years older than I am, but I always catch up with her. She'll be seventeen next month, and in another month after that, I'll be sixteen."

Now that we knew who they were, the girls abandoned their defiant attitude and talked to us freely about themselves and their parents. They had lived in several places, but what they remembered best was the home in which they had been so happy with their mother and daddy. They described a lovely old house surrounded by trees under which they played in summer and which their mother said "obligingly" shed their leaves in winter so that the sunshine could brighten the big rooms of the house. They had a Persian cat, named "Whiskers," and their daddy said he sounded "just like an outboard motor" when he sat in front of the open fire on winter evenings, purring in happy contentment. Their dog was supposed to be a hunting dog, and he had papers and a long name, but they called him "Hun" and petted him so much that he stopped being a hunting dog. Their father said he didn't mind, because he didn't want to go hunting without their mother, and she didn't like the idea of killing any living thing.

Their father used to pretend he was a horse and give them rides on his back, and when people asked him if he hadn't ordered one of them to be a boy, he always answered, "Who wants a nasty boy?" He usually added much more, about not being willing to swap his two little girls for all the boys in the world.

Their mother sewed beautifully, and she made them pretty dresses and all sorts of lovely underthings. She called them her "two little dolls." Once she made costumes for their dolls, "dresses and hats and everything" exactly like theirs, and their father said, "Now you have four little dolls." They could still remember how their mother laughed at that and how it delighted their father to hear her laugh. Then they added a little wistfully, "We loved to hear her too."

They could think of nothing that they wished for in those days that they didn't have except a "grandma." When they were "real little" somebody had asked them one Christmas what they wanted Santa Claus to bring them. They had both said, "a grandmother." That was because "Wendy," the little girl next door, had such a nice grandmother. She made delicious cookies and candies, and she was never cross when Wendy's parents went out at night and she had to stay with her.

But they had no grandparents "on either side." When their parents went out, Mamie, who was their housekeeper, had to stay with them. At first, she just used to fuss about people having children and not being willing to stay home with them. As time went on, she said more and more, and they began to understand that some of the things she was saying about their mother weren't "nice." They often wished she'd go away and leave them by themselves.

Then came the dark days, which they didn't like to remember. Their father's business took him away quite often, and whenever he returned, there was quarreling between him and their mother. They didn't know who was right; they couldn't believe either of them was wrong, but it was "terrible" to hear them speak to each other the way they did. They heard Mamie tell Cook and the laundryman that their mother was to blame and that she'd seen it coming and could have told Mr. Abbott about it long ago, only she didn't want to make trouble.

It was Mamie who broke the news to them that their father and mother were going to separate. They might have understood what that meant if they had listened carefully to all that she said, but she talked so much that they paid little attention to her. They were totally unprepared for the question put to them by the Divorce Court. "Would you rather live with your father or your mother?" The only answer that either of them could give was "both." The old judge shook his finger at them and told them they would have to choose one or the other of their parents; they were "separating," and the children couldn't live with both of them because their mother was going away to live in another city and their father would continue to live in the same place. This should have made it clear, but the children persisted in saying that they wanted to live with both their parents. Mae said, "I guess he thought we were stupid. But he was the stupid one because he couldn't understand that we meant we wanted our parents to stay together, and we wanted to stay with them."

The Judge finally threw up his hands and said, "Well, I can't cut them in half, and I don't intend to separate them. The only thing I can do is to award custody to the mother for the first six months of every year and to the father for the remaining six months. If the parties wish to arrange it otherwise for their convenience, let that be a matter of agreement between them. But each of the parents is to have custody of the children for six months out of each year."

Mae was then seven years old, and Sadie was eight, and they had only a vague idea of what the judge had decided. They soon found out, for "right off the bat" their father and mother agreed that their father should have them first, instead of their mother.

Their mother said she would stay with them for a few days "to check over their things," and their father said he would stay at the hotel until she was ready to leave. They couldn't understand why their father should go to a hotel instead of going home with them; and their mother's explanation, "He can't, because I'm going to be there," didn't make things any clearer. Nor did they understand half of the other things she told them during the days which intervened before she left. She tried to make them see that it was "for the best" for her and their daddy to separate. She said the "continual nagging and quarreling" was bad for them. They assured her that they didn't mind it, and they pleaded with her not to leave. When it was time for her to go, they thought she might have changed her mind if their daddy had said something nice when he called instead of just asking her when she was leaving. She said "right away," and she was gone almost before they knew it.

Mamie stayed on, becoming worse than ever. She said she was "boss" now, and one of the first things she did was to get rid of Whiskers. She hated cats, and it "made her blood run cold" if Whiskers happened to touch her. She didn't like dogs either, and she kept after the children's father until he sent Hun away. She ran the house, and she "ran" them and their daddy until they were all miserable. Nothing seemed to be right any more, and they didn't wonder that their father stopped coming home to dinner. Mamie prepared only what she herself liked to eat, and it was usually the same thing every day.

Sadie and Mae no longer looked like "little dolls." Their cheeks were not round and rosy, and their hair looked scraggly and untidy. Mamie kept them clean, but she didn't bother to press their dresses; and if a button came off, it was never sewed on again. It was a long time before their father noticed anything, and when he did, he asked, "Mamie, what's the matter with the kids? They don't look like the same children." Mamie replied that they were growing, but that didn't seem to satisfy him. He was home for dinner for a while after that, and they tried to eat a little more to please him. Sadie "guessed" it was their fault that he started staying out again, because they talked too much about their mother. They couldn't talk to Mamie about her because they knew she "hated" their mother, and they were so lonesome for her that they just had to talk to somebody.

When their father told Mamie not to expect him for dinner unless he called up, Mamie took advantage of the situation by feeding the children early and putting them to bed before dark. They couldn't sleep, and they stayed in bed only until they were sure that Mamie had left the house. Then they got up and did as they pleased until they heard her return. She caught them up a couple of times and gave them a "good whacking," but they were glad she didn't tell their father. He found it out for himself by coming home unexpectedly early one night. Sadie and Mae had been in the living room in their pajamas, and they were starting to run up the stairs when their father switched on the light. He called to them, and they were delighted to find that it was he and not Mamie. They ran down again and kissed him, saying, "We're so glad it's you." And when he asked them who they thought it was, they said, "Mamie."

He went up to their room with them and asked them how often Mamie went out and left them alone. When they told him "nearly every night," he was furious and said he could hardly wait until Mamie got back so that he could "bawl her out." But after a while he quieted down and sat for a long time with Mae on one knee and Sadie on the other and an arm around each of them. When Mamie came home, he told her very calmly that he should have known that it was asking too much to expect her to stay with the children every night; but since he didn't realize it, she should have told him and not just gone out and left them alone. He said things couldn't go on the way they were because anybody could see the children weren't being properly cared for. He gave Mamie two weeks' notice.

Mamie left the next day, and their father stayed home from the office the following day. He said he was going to pack their clothes, but he found that all the lovely things their mother had made for them were in an "unsightly" condition. He took them downtown and bought them everything they needed. It was the first time they had been shopping since their mother left, and they had a "grand time." The dresses they bought were so large that they "swallowed them up," but their father said there was no time for alterations. When they asked him why, he said, "Because I'm putting you on the evening train. I'm sending you to your mother."

It was a wonderful trip, and the eyes of both girls sparkled with pleasure as they told us about it. Even though they were placed in charge of the Pullman conductor, they felt that they were traveling alone. They had dinner in the dining car and ordered everything that wasn't good for them. When it was time to go to bed, a lady who had an upper berth swapped with them so that they could climb up "the cute little ladder." They let a pretty young lady comb their hair and help them to dress, just as though they hadn't been doing such things for themselves ever since their mother had left. Everybody on the train was very nice to them, and they "were too happy for anything" because they were going to see their mother.

She was standing on the platform when they reached their destination. They saw her immediately and wanted to jump to her through the window. It seemed to them that it was "ages" before all the baggage was unloaded and the people started to get off the train. Even then, they had to wait until the conductor was ready to go with them. They pointed out their mother to him, but she had to show him "lots of papers" before he "delivered" them.

It was three months since they had last seen her, long months which had seemed like years to the lonely children. But they thought the time must have passed quickly for their mother, for she asked why their father had sent them "so soon." She didn't wait for an answer before she asked with a rippling laugh, "Wherever did you get those over-sized dresses?" When they told her they had gone shopping with their father and selected the dresses themselves, she laughed again. "That's just what they look like."

She called a taxi, and as their bags were being put in, Mae told her mother that everything in them was "brand new." When they were all seated in the cab, their mother wanted to know if they had outgrown all their clothes, and Sadie told her that Mamie hadn't been taking care of their things and that their father had said they looked like "orphans." They also told how Mamie treated them and how their father had got angry when he discovered that she was leaving them alone at night. After that their mother was very quiet and didn't laugh again until the taxi stopped in front of a tall building and Mae asked if that "big house" was hers. Then she was her old gay self again and said, "No, Goosie, that's not a house at all. It's an apartment building, and all I have is a tiny little nest in the very top of that tall tree."

The children had never seen anything like their mother's penthouse apartment. One side of the long living room was glass, and the dining room was round, with ladies and men who were half undressed painted on the wall. Their mother's bedroom was all dainty ruffles and ribbons and looked like the pictures in their fairy book. But what delighted them most was the terrace. It was lined with beautiful flowers, all in bloom, and it was so high up that the people walking down on the sidewalk looked like little dwarfs. On clear days they could see the white cap of a distant mountain peak, and at night they could look up and see the stars and look down and see thousands of lights twinkling in the city below them.

Their mother washed their hair and curled it and "took in" their new dresses and shortened them. She slept in one of the twin beds in her room, and they were both supposed to sleep in the other. The beds were separated by only a small night table, but they couldn't bear to be even that far away from her, and so they begged every night to be permitted to sleep in the same bed with her. It was a little crowded, but she let them have their way about this and about almost everything else during the first week after their arrival.

She didn't tell them anything about their "new daddy" until the morning of the day he came home. Then she said his name was "Bob," and he was very nice, and she hoped they would like him. They didn't want any "new daddy," and they couldn't see why their own daddy couldn't come and live there with their mother and them and let their "new daddy" go elsewhere. She told them not to talk like that, and they said no more about it because they didn't want to displease her. They hoped that Bob would be something like their own daddy, and they were disappointed when he turned out "as different as could be."

Their mother had them all dressed up and looking their best when he arrived, but the effort was wasted on him. All he wanted to know was "where in hell" they had come from and why their mother hadn't told him. She explained that she didn't know they were coming until she received a wire from their father saying that he had put them on the train. Then he "blew up" and called their father all kinds of "bad names" and wanted to know how long they were going to stay. When their mother replied, "About six months," he declared that he'd be "damned" if he'd keep them longer than their own father had. He said there was no room for them in the apartment, and he'd like to know where they were going to sleep. Their mother had thought they could use the big couch in the living room, but Bob said that wouldn't work because company dropped in almost every night. It ended up with the children sleeping in their mother's bed for the first part of the night and then transferring to the living room when Bob and their mother retired. They didn't mind the arrangement if only Bob hadn't started fussing and cursing in the middle of the night about their being such a "nuisance."

Their mother was always telling them that they had to be nice to Bob if they wanted to stay there. They did want to stay with her, but they could see that Bob didn't like them. The only time he looked at them was one day when he came home early and their mother was out. They had been playing at gardening on the terrace, and they were very dirty, and the wind had blown their hair "to pieces." Of course he "would" choose a time like that to look them over from head to foot.

When their mother came home, he said, "They must look like their father. They certainly don't resemble you in the least."

They soon learned that the best thing they could do was to keep out of Bob's way as much as possible. They asked their mother to let them have their dinner in the kitchen before Bob came home in the evening. Then they went out on the terrace and stayed there until it was time to go to bed. But they could be with their mother during the day, and that made up for everything that was unpleasant about the evenings.

When three months had passed, their stepfather insisted that their mother put them on the train and wire their father that she was sending them, just as he had done. This was a cruel blow to the children because they had been "awfully good." Of course they would be glad to see their father again, but he had to work all day, and they knew he couldn't be with them very much. They heard their mother telling Bob how much they wanted to stay, but he wouldn't hear of it.

Their father was still living in the old house, and he did the best he could for them when they got back. He sent them to a private school and arranged for them to stay there in the afternoon and study their lessons for the next day. He picked them up on his way home from the office and took them to a restaurant for dinner. Sometimes they went to a movie, but usually they went home right after dinner. They had an old woman who cleaned the house and did the laundry, but she didn't have anything to do with the children. Their father stayed with them at night, and he got up in the morning and prepared breakfast for them. He still had to go away on business sometimes, and when that happened, he sent his secretary, Miss Phipps, to stay with them.

He wrote to their mother and told her that they were getting along fairly well and that it might be advisable for them to stay with him until the end of the school term, to avoid having to change schools in the middle of the year. She agreed to this, but when it was time for them to go to her, she couldn't take them because she was going to Europe with Bob. There was another delay when she got back, and they had been with their father more than a year before they went back to their mother.

Bob was just as disagreeable as ever, continually nagging their mother about them. They couldn't stay out on the terrace because it was cold now, and, besides, they had to do their lessons. The maid didn't want them in the kitchen, but they stayed there anyway whenever Bob was home. They finally asked their mother to let them go back to their father, although they had been with her only six months and it was "her turn" to keep them for a year. They loved her just as much as ever, but they knew Bob didn't want them in his home, and they could see that he was making things miserable for their mother on account of them.

Then something happened that changed their whole lives. When they went back to their father, he told them he was glad to have them, but he didn't see how he could go on as he had the last time. He asked them how they would like to have a "new mother" to keep house for them. When they thought about their experience with their "new daddy," they answered, "No" very emphatically. But he said they were "getting big," and he didn't see how he could make a home for them unless he remarried. He asked them how they liked Miss Phipps; when they both said they didn't like her, he was sorry because he had already asked her to marry him, and she had accepted him.

Miss Phipps talked a lot about "making a home" for them, and she was better than Mamie about sewing on buttons and taking care of their clothes. But when their father came home in the evening, he had to kiss her first, even if they were standing in the door waiting for him. She was very nice to them when their father was around, but they knew she didn't really like them, and she was jealous of everything their father did for them. She was even more jealous of their mother, and she flew into a rage one day when they said they wished their father and mother would go back together again.

Although she was not as outspoken as Bob, they soon discovered that she didn't want them in their father's home any more than their stepfather wanted them in their mother's home. They were shunted back and forth at irregular intervals, and they didn't blame either their mother or their father because they realized that they no longer belonged in the home of either of them.

When Mae was twelve and Sadie was thirteen years old, a little stepbrother arrived to "bless" the home of their father. Not very long after that, their stepmother insisted on having a "modern" house, and their father moved away from the old home. As time went on, Miss Phipps didn't even pretend to be nice to them. She frequently asked their father to send them back to their mother before it was time for them to go, but Bob always refused to let their mother take them until it was "her turn." Their father and mother discussed the matter for hours at a time over the long-distance telephone, and they finally agreed that there was only one thing to do and that was to place the girls in a boarding school.

Sadie and Mae met many girls in the boarding school who had been placed there because they were "incorrigible" and many others who were unwanted by their parents for various reasons. Although they were all children who didn't "belong" anywhere else, they resented the fact that they were there, and they vented their dissatisfaction upon all those about them. Sadie and Mae were very unhappy, and they soon fell into the general pattern of resentfulness and contemptuous defiance. They were punished nearly all the time they were there. This meant that their parents were requested not to visit them, and they were denied the privilege of going home for holidays. When this brought no improvement in their attitude, the privilege of corresponding with their parents, though always subject to censorship, was withdrawn entirely.

Some of the other girls went home or to camp for the summer vacation, but Sadie and Mae remained in the boarding school "for three straight years." When they could bear it no longer, they decided to run away, but they laid their plans carefully to avoid being caught and brought back. Their experience in traveling back and forth between the homes of their parents enabled them to make their way to different places; and by adopting different names in every place, they managed to evade the authorities all over the country.

When they came to our city, they found employment as "B-Drinkers" in one of the cabarets of the French Quarter. They were told that all they had to do was to consume quantities of "soft drinks" every night and "kid the guys who were paying for them into thinking they were drinking liquor." It looked like an easy way to make twenty or thirty dollars a night, even when they learned about some of the other "angles." These were the big parties "thrown" for important people, held in private rooms where the "B-Drinkers" had to sit on men's laps and do everything else to please the "honored guests."

One of these honored guests must have been honorable as well as honored, for instead of reveling in the youth and charm of the girls who had been provided for the gratification of his senses, he noticed that they looked like "decent kids," and he reported their presence in the "night spot" to the police.

The proprietor produced the birth certificates which the girls had furnished when they were employed and which showed them to be over eighteen years of age. This might have ended the matter if the detective who was sent out on the case hadn't happened to have two little daughters of his own. He looked at the girls, and he looked at the certificates again, and he said, "They may be over eighteen, but they don't look it. I'll have to check into this matter further."

He went to the address which they had given the night club proprietor as their residence, and he learned from their landlady that the birth certificates belonged to her daughters and that Sadie and Mae must have stolen them. When they still refused to give the detective their correct names, he had brought them in to us, and we then succeeded in locating their parents.

Under the prevailing practice we could have shipped Mae and Sadie back to their home state, to be dealt with there by the authorities. But after hearing their story, we wanted to do something more than that for them.

We sent for their father and stepmother, and for their mother and stepfather. They all came except Bob, the stepfather.

We talked to the parents long and earnestly and tried to make them see how much their girls needed them and how disastrous would be the consequences if they failed them again. When they suggested a better boarding school, we told them that no boarding school would be "better" for their girls. What they needed was a home where they could feel that they belonged.

The father said he loved his daughters dearly; he was "cut-up" over what had happened to them. He was willing to try them in his home again, but he was afraid it wouldn't work. After talking to his second wife out of his presence we were convinced that the girls had been right about the feelings of jealousy and animosity, which she tried to conceal from her husband, but which were apparently just as strong as ever.

Then we conferred with the mother and we told her that, in our opinion, she was the only person who could give the girls what they needed. She wanted to do anything she could, but she had never been able to get her second husband to accept her children, and she was afraid he might be worse, now that they had been in trouble.

We sent for the girls, and we saw much evidence of the strong bond of affection which still existed between them and their parents. Tears were flowing freely as we left them together, telling them to talk it over while we handled some other cases.

When we returned, the girls said their mother was willing to take them back, and they wanted to be with her more than anything in the world, but they didn't think they could ever feel they belonged in Bob's home.

This reminded their father that Sadie and Mae now owned a house of their own. He said it was an old-fashioned cottage, but in good repair and fully furnished. It had been held in trust for the girls; the old grandaunt who had the use of it during her lifetime had died recently, and the girls now had a clear title to it. As their legal guardian, their father had intended to sell it and invest the proceeds for them. When he reached this point, the girls cried out in unison, "Oh, please, Daddy, don't sell it. Let us keep it and live in it."

We said nothing to dampen their enthusiasm for a while, because we wanted the parents to see just how much a home meant to the girls. When this had been accomplished, we said regretfully that it was a pity that the girls were much too young to live alone. They broke down and cried bitterly at this, and though we have witnessed it many hundreds of times, we have never yet been able to steel ourselves against the devastating grief of youth. Unlike the sorrow of their elders, which is often tempered by the hand of time, the grief of youth is pure and unalloyed by any doubt as to the worth of what is lost. We saw the father and mother trying to resist, but we knew they couldn't. They were deeply moved, and tears of love and sympathy were still in their eyes when the girls' sobbing finally subsided and Mae tried to smile and say lightly, "We always wanted a grandmother. If we had one now, she could come and live in our house with us." Then the mother's bright laugh rang out and cleared the atmosphere almost instantly, as she said, "You little goosie, you don't need any grandmother. Your mother is going to live in that beautiful old house with you. And she's never going to leave you again." And when Sadie asked, "What about Bob?" she answered, "You can invite him to come live with us in your house if you like. But it'll be your house, and if he doesn't behave, you can ask him how long he's going to stay."

This was what the girls had been wanting for so many years, and we had high hopes that they weren't getting it too late, as we listened to the merry laughter which rang out as their mother said, "And I can tell you another thing. When you girls get married and have children, they're going to have a grandmother."

11

SYLVIA

The first we heard of either Sylvia or her family was
through an anonymous telephone call. Before the Police
Department set up a special section to handle juveniles,
all reports concerning children came directly to the
Court. Ordinarily our Chief Probation Officer required
informants to give their names and addresses before we
would listen to complaints. He and his one assistant
were carrying a case load which would have taxed the
capacity of a half-dozen workers. In addition, the "Chief"
had to handle all intake. He had neither time nor facilities to take proper care of all the cases reported by responsible individuals and agencies. From experience he
knew that anonymous telephone calls led him on a "wild
goose chase" more often than not.

In every way that he knew he tried to obtain the name
of the caller. He assured her that we would respect her
confidence—if she would just let us know where we
could reach her. We wanted to check with her, if necessary, after looking into the matter. All she would say
was that she was calling for someone else who had seen
"the three children in the shed" and who didn't want to

get involved. She didn't even know the exact location of the shed. When the Probation Officer pressed her for more details, he found that she had hung up. He wondered afterwards, and probably still wonders, if he wouldn't have done better to have hung up on her when she refused to give her name and address. As it was, she hadn't told him enough to enable him to turn the matter over to his assistant. Yet, she had told him too much to permit him to forget it and wait for it to be reported by someone else. There was nothing to do but drop everything and go out and look for the children.

He stuck his head in his assistant's office, asked her to "hold things down" until he returned, and was on his way. He knew the streets so well that he was able to avoid congested parts of the city, quickly getting out to the suburb in which he believed the shed to be located. The information that had been given him was vague, but he knew he had to look for a dirt road leading off the main highway, with a "No Dumping" sign at the entrance. He found any number of such roads, each with its "No Dumping" sign. He tried each in turn. They were all so rough and bumpy that he thought his old car would be shaken to pieces before he found the right road.

When he did find it, it was indistinguishable from the others except that its "No Dumping" sign was a little more battered. Turning into the road and traveling a few hundred feet, he saw what looked like a row of shacks behind a high pile of trash. He stopped his car and walked over to the shacks, but he saw no living creature anywhere in the vicinity. He was looking at the mountainous heap of garbage, making a mental note of the fact that people with trash to dump evidently didn't believe in signs, when he made out the figure of an old woman dressed in rags which made her almost indistinguishable from the pile of garbage from which she was emerging. He made his way to her and asked if she had seen anything of three children.

She was so deaf that it was hard for her to hear what the Probation Officer was asking. It was even harder for him to understand the answers which came from her toothless mouth. He finally learned that a woman with three children had lived in one of the shacks for about a week and had left the day before. She had gone to work in a dairy. The old woman was willing to go with the Probation Officer and show him where the dairy was, provided he would bring her back.

He helped her into his car and tried to follow her directions, but she was a poor guide, and they went miles out of their way before they arrived at the dairy. The old woman got out and led him down the middle of a large, well-lighted barn with long rows of cows on each side. When they reached the end, they came to a small woman sitting on a stool and milking one of the cows. The old woman called to her. "Hattie, there's a gentleman here to see you." She replied, without looking up from her task. "Can't you see I'm stripping? I'm late already, and I can't talk to nobody till I get done."

The Probation Officer looked at his watch. It was after four o'clock, and he knew there was work waiting for him in his office. But he waited. Probably, he thought, Hattie was the mother of the children for whom he had been looking all day. He walked around the dairy and noticed milking machines and modern equipment, and yet he saw that Hattie had to work very hard to get that last thin stream of milk from the udder of each cow.

When she had finished, she came up to them, wiping her hands on her apron and saying, "I'm slow because I'm a little out of practice. My hands are stiff. But when I get the hang of it again, it won't take me that long to strip thirty-four cows."

She led them into the milk room, and the Probation Officer found that she was quite willing to answer questions while she was operating the bottling machine. She said the three children in the shack were hers. They had stayed there a week because she had just arrived in town and had no place else to go and no money to buy food. She made it clear that she "knew her way around." Experience had taught her the advantages of locating near a garbage dump. "You can always get enough to eat off a dump like that. People throw away cans nearly full of good food." She also confided to the officer that she had learned that it does no good to ask for charity, "unless you want somebody to tell you how to live your life."

The Officer told her that he was interested in the children. She said they would be all right now that she had been lucky enough to get this job. It was hard work—she knew that when she took it—but it paid well, and the children had a good roof over their heads. "I didn't fool myself. I knew it was hard work and long hours every day, not leaving out Sundays and holidays. But I'm making good money, and I've got a nice room with two big beds in the main house. The kids get plenty to eat and have the run of the whole place. They're better off now than they've ever been."

The Probation Officer talked to Mrs. Brown, Hattie's employer, who confirmed everything Hattie had told him about the arrangements for the children. She had no children of her own. Hattie's children, she said, would never want for anything as long as they were there.

The little boy was on the porch playing with a dog, and the girls were in the kitchen, where they had been watching Mrs. Brown make a cake. They were not very responsive when the Officer tried to talk to them, and they all looked painfully thin and pale.

Because it was late, the Officer contented himself with getting the names and ages of the children and a few other details. He found that Eddie, who was the youngest child, was four years old. Next to him was Beverly, who was six, exactly one year younger than the oldest child, Sylvia, who was seven.

When the Officer was leaving, he told Hattie that he would send his assistant to see her within the next few days, and he hoped Hattie would cooperate. Hattie agreed to see her, but she couldn't imagine what more they wanted of her. The Officer explained it was his duty to make sure that the children were being properly cared for. He gently reminded her that they had spent a week in an open shed beside a garbage dump. At this she flared up and said she had been caring for the children ever since they were born and nobody was going to tell her how to do it. He told her that he was sorry if anything he had said offended her, but he felt that it would be necessary to go into the matter a little further.

His assistant came the next day and got enough facts about the children and their mother to write a brief case history. She learned the mother had been legally married to the father of the two girls, but she had no idea of his whereabouts, for she hadn't seen him since before Beverly was born. The boy was illegitimate, and Hattie frankly admitted that she didn't know who his father was.

Hattie was asked to take the children to a clinic for a check-up. Although her employer said she could get off any morning, she broke all the appointments we made for her. Our Officer finally took them to the clinic himself. After the examinations and tests had been completed, we received a report showing that all the children were suffering from malnutrition, dating probably from infancy.

Hattie showed little interest in the high caloric diet recommended by the doctors even though Mrs. Brown agreed to provide it. Nor did she think it important to clean the children's heads, even when told the clinic report showed they were infested with pediculosis to an extent that it possibly was impairing the children's health. Again, Mrs. Brown came to the rescue and, under the direction of our Officer, she succeeded in eradicating the trouble.

Shortly after this Hattie asked our Officer not to talk to Mrs. Brown about the children. This was a new development. Hattie had previously referred us to her employer for confirmation of her statements about the good care the children were receiving. We were concerned about her change of attitude because we had been depending on Mrs. Brown to see that measures recommended for the children's welfare were being carried out. We conferred with Mrs. Brown and learned that she had noticed that Hattie was beginning to resent anything she did for the children. Hattie accused her of trying to buy the children's affection with new clothes and all sorts of "fancy things" she couldn't afford.

We tried to explain Mrs. Brown's interest in the children to Hattie by telling her that it was only natural that she should like them and want to help them since she was a motherly person without any children of her own to look after. But Hattie's answer was always the same. "Let Mrs. Brown go and get some children the way I did if she wants them. She's not going to steal mine."

When Hattie came to the Court and said she was going to give up her job and place the children in a "home," we didn't try to dissuade her, although we were doubtful about the children's eligibility for institutional placement. In view of the rule that when there is a living parent, such placement will be made only at the request of the parent, we sent the mother to the agency which handled intake for the only institution available to children of their age and religion. The agency advised Hattie not to apply for institutional placement because of the children's need for a special diet and other factors which indicated they could not meet the standards of the institution.

When Hattie came back to us and told us they had turned her down, we sent her to another agency to apply for foster home placement. We thought she understood what was meant by foster home placement, since we had explained it to her at great length when she said she didn't want the children adopted. The agency thought Hattie still didn't understand, and so they explained it to her all over again and even took her to visit one of their foster homes so that she could see just what it was like.

When Hattie saw children living happily in a foster home with parents who weren't theirs, she concluded that it would be no better than where they were because she feared her children would think more of the foster parents than they did of her. She much preferred an institution because she felt sure there would be no one there to take her place in the children's hearts. The agency worker explained to us that it would be impossible to get any foster mother to keep the children if Hattie resisted this type of placement.

The worker felt confident, however, of being able to change Hattie's attitude. She made frequent visits to the dairy and talked to Hattie long and earnestly about the welfare of her children. Mrs. Brown also tried to persuade Hattie to try the foster home by telling her that if there was anything about it she didn't like, the agency would transfer the children to another foster home. Hattie then accused her employer of wanting to get rid of the children. The employer said that she would be willing to keep both Hattie and the children if only Hattie would act differently.

Hattie became even more difficult as time went on. We knew that Mrs. Brown was putting up with her only because she felt sorry for the children, and we were beginning to see that Hattie could never part with her children voluntarily. Therefore we offered to remove them forcibly if any placement could be found. But no agency, either public or private, would accept them on this basis. Having no facilities of our own, all the Court could do was wait and hope that Hattie could be induced to consent to foster home placement.

During all these negotiations, Mrs. Brown cooperated with us fully. At our suggestion she discontinued her attentions to the children. This proved very difficult since she was really fond of them, and they naturally turned to her for the love and affection which their overwrought mother was unable to give. Sylvia, who had always been her mother's favorite, now stayed away from her mother more and more. She told Mrs. Brown that she couldn't

bear the cross looks and harsh words, which were all that
her mother seemed to have for her.

Young as she was, Sylvia sensed the growing resentment between Mrs. Brown and her mother. She loved
both of them, and she wished there was something she
could do to make them like each other. She could think
of nothing until she heard that Mrs. Brown was going
to have a birthday. All the children had had birthdays
since they were there, and Mrs. Brown had bought each
of them a lovely present. Hattie had said that was why
the children liked Mrs. Brown, and now Sylvia's childish
mind conceived a plan to make her mother and Mrs.
Brown like each other.

She didn't dare ask Hattie to buy a present for Mrs.
Brown. She decided that she would buy the present
and then ask Hattie to give it to Mrs. Brown. Carefully
she extracted three one-dollar bills from the shoe box in
which Hattie kept her money. The next time the agency
worker took her downtown for a test she asked to go to
a department store to make a purchase. It took her quite
a while to find something for three dollars that would
be nice enough for Mrs. Brown, but when she saw a box
of brightly colored handkerchiefs, she knew it would be
just the thing.

When she got home, her mother was "stripping." Sylvia was so eager to show her the handkerchiefs that she
forgot to be afraid of the scolding she always received
for going into the dairy. She went straight to Hattie and,
opening the box, told her to look at the lovely present she
had bought for her to give Mrs. Brown. Hattie stared at
the child in amazement, and her voice was hoarse with
anger as she gasped, "You get out of here. I don't want to
give that woman nothing." Sylvia moved back a little

before she said, "But she's going to have a birthday,
Mama." Hattie jumped up, overturning both her stool
and the bucket of milk. She grasped Sylvia by both
shoulders and almost shook the breath out of her body
as she asked, "Where did you get the money to buy that
trash?" Sylvia couldn't answer, but she managed to nod
her head when her mother said, "You got it out of my box!
You stole my hard-earned money to buy that woman a
present!"

Now Hattie vented all her pent-up resentment against
the whole world upon her poor, defenseless child. She
picked up a piece of rubber hose and beat Sylvia until
she was senseless. Then she realized what she had done,
and she threw the hose to the other end of the dairy.
She waited a few minutes to see if Sylvia would "wake
up," and then she lifted her in her arms and carried her
to Mrs. Brown, screaming, "Oh, look what I've done.
Please do something for my baby, and I'll never be ugly
to you again, Mrs. Brown."

Mrs. Brown laid the child on her bed and felt her
pulse, and then she said, as gently as she could, "I'm
afraid it's too late, Hattie. But I'll call the ambulance."

Sylvia's death was due to "shock and multiple contu-
sions," according to the report of the coroner's inquest.
The newspapers headlined the story and Hattie was besieged with reporters. When placed on the defensive,
she said that she had only been trying to "correct" her
child and that this was not the first time Sylvia had stolen
from her. She said she didn't know a piece of hose could
hurt that much because she used it on the cows all the
time and they didn't even seem to feel it. She also said
that she had never before "placed a finger" on any of her
children.

When Mrs. Brown was interviewed, she reluctantly admitted that the children "were inclined to pick things up," but she had never mentioned it to the social worker or to our officer because "Hattie had asked her not to." She didn't think it was anything serious anyway. She believed it was just a habit they had developed from living near dumps, where anything they could find was theirs for the taking. She confirmed Hattie's statement that this was the first time she had "corrected" any of the children.

Hattie was arrested and charged with "murder in the first degree." A lunacy commission appointed by the Criminal Court found Hattie "sane," according to the legal definition of the term. The attorney appointed by the Court to represent Hattie based her defense on lack of malice in that she was merely exercising her right and performing her duty as a parent in disciplining her child for "stealing."

The jury found Hattie guilty of murder but recommended clemency. The Court accepted the jury's recommendation and sentenced Hattie to the State Penitentiary for a term of not less than three, and not more than five, years. Mrs. Brown was willing to have the two younger children remain in her home if Hattie wanted her to keep them until she was released from prison. But Hattie didn't, and the institution which had previously turned them down now yielded to the pressure of public opinion and an indignant press and accepted them for placement.

Was the institution wrong in having refused to take the children when Hattie wanted to place them? The answer is "No," if you consider that it is impossible for an institution to do the best possible job for the average child if it accepts children who cannot measure up to standards in matters of health, behavior, and educability. But the answer is "Yes," if you consider that in this particular case the institution was the only facility available for the placement of Hattie's children.

12

TRAGIC BEAUTY

The petition which was handed to us as Marie and Stephanie came into the Hearing Room gave their ages as fifteen and sixteen respectively. Although juveniles frequently misrepresent their age to arresting officers, it is almost invariably by adding years rather than by subtracting them. But Marie, the younger girl, looked all of twenty, and Stephanie could have passed for twenty-five.

In their folder we saw that the ages had been verified. We also saw that the girls had been born in our city, and we recognized their surname as that of one of the oldest and most aristocratic families in the state.

Both girls were tall and stately, with a natural poise and grace of bearing which impressed all who saw them. They were immaculately groomed and so strikingly beautiful that they looked as though they might have stepped out of some exquisite painting.

Marie was dressed in black, with soft, white chiffon ruffles at her throat and wrists. Her dark hair and luminous black eyes contrasted sharply with the ivory whiteness of her smooth young skin. Her sister Stephanie

presented an equally enchanting picture in the deep purple costume which accentuated the blue of her eyes and
heightened the lustre of her bronze hair. Both girls had
fine, clearly chiseled features and well-molded figures.
And they were also possessed of a charming manner of
quiet confidence and assurance which never deserted
them.

Everything about them bespoke proud ancestry and
gentle breeding. We were not surprised to learn that
their father, Edmond, was a scion of the distinguished
family whose name they bore. Like many of the sons of
our "oldest and best families," he had scorned prepara-
tion for any career other than an artistic one, even though
his parents could ill afford the expense of sending him
abroad and keeping him there for several years. They
managed it by depriving themselves of almost everything
which was not essential for "keeping up appearances."
But when it was time for his two sisters to make their
debut into society, Edmond had to come home. His parents realized that, by bringing him back to this country
before he had "made his mark" in Paris or London, they
were making it difficult for him to achieve success as an
artist at home. But they had no alternative, for the
family would need every penny it could muster to present their daughters to society and afford them an opportunity to make good marriages. It would also be desirable to have Edmond on hand to help his father in all
the intrigue and manipulations which would be necessary to accomplish the all-important feat of having his
sisters chosen members of the "courts" of the mock royalty
which reigned over the Mardi Gras balls. As an eligible
bachelor he would also be a welcome addition to the
numerous debutante parties given for his sisters by rela-

tives and old friends of the family. There was the added possibility that, by returning home while he was still young and handsome, Edmond might be able to gratify his desire to devote his life to art by making a match with the daughter of some parvenu who would be willing to exchange some of his wealth for the prestige and social standing of Edmond's family.

Edmond arrived home on the day of his sisters' coming out party. He was a great disappointment to the entire family, for he brought with him a wife, whom he had picked up in the demimonde of Paris. Her name was Colette, and she had been the toast of one of the dives of Montmartre frequented by young artists. Edmond would probably never have married her if he hadn't been compelled to leave Paris just as he was becoming interested in her.

The family never accepted her, but she made him a much better wife than he had any right to expect. She was a thrifty housekeeper, and she stretched Edmond's small income so as to cover all their expenses. She was also an excellent cook, and the delicious meals which she prepared for Edmond were the equal of those he had enjoyed during the years he spent in Paris. Under Colette's management he was able to devote himself to his art as wholeheartedly as though he had married a wealthy heiress.

She presented him with five beautiful daughters in as many years. It was not until she died giving birth to the last of them that he realized how much she had done for him. When he hired a housekeeper and tried to continue his way of life, he found it impossible. The housekeeper spent a month's income in a week and made no attempt to keep the children from annoying him when he was at work.

When the family learned that he was considering placing the children in an orphan asylum, they were horrified; and when he asked them what else he could do, they reluctantly suggested that he "go into business." He didn't know the first thing about business, but he did succeed in getting a job with an advertising agency. It was very distasteful to him; he called it prostituting his art. It was still difficult for him to "make both ends meet," but he attributed this to the extravagance of his housekeepers, whom he was continually changing in the hope of finding one who could manage as well as Colette.

The children grew "like weeds," and although they were neglected in many ways, they were all very attractive. However, Stephanie, who was the eldest, and Marie, who was one year younger, were headstrong and impudent. They did exactly as they pleased, and several of the housekeepers told their father that they were incorrigible. This was also the opinion of Edmond's family, who said that the older girls "took after their mother."

Edmond struggled along for several years and was getting deeper and deeper into debt when he was offered a position with one of the top advertising agencies in New York. The salary was very attractive, but Edmond hesitated about accepting it on account of his children. His mother had died, and although several members of the family were willing to take the three younger children, none of them would have anything to do with the two older girls.

He delayed as long as he could, but his financial condition finally made it necessary for him to take the New York position. He placed the three younger children with his sisters and left Stephanie and Marie in the charge of "Clementine," an old mulatto woman who had been attached to the family for years. He asked the relatives to "keep an eye" on the girls, and although they refused, he felt sure they would.

Clementine adored both of "her young ladies." She waited on them "hand and foot" and did their bidding at all times of the night and day. She didn't keep the house very clean because she knew they didn't care anything about that. But she looked after their clothes and acted as personal maid. She served their breakfast in bed every morning, and when they were ready to get up, usually about noon, they called to her to get their baths ready for them. She knew they should be going to school, but school was almost out by the time they had finished dressing.

When the family heard how things were going, they sent for Clementine and told her she was ruining the girls; she should make them go to school. When Clementine went home and told Marie and Stephanie what their relatives had said, they just laughed and told Clementine she didn't have to worry about their schooling as they knew enough already. Clementine realized that they did know how to "fix themselves up," and she always said they "looked like a million dollars" when they went out. She felt in her heart that girls who were as beautiful as they shouldn't have to study too much.

As a matter of fact, they were very well informed, in spite of their lack of formal education. They could converse intelligently on almost any subject, and their diction and vocabularies were superior to those of many college graduates. No one understood how they had learned what they knew because they were never seen reading or doing anything else to improve their minds.

From early childhood, they had enjoyed but one pastime and that was "dressing up." As they grew up they devoted themselves more and more to the adornment of their persons. It was apparently their one interest in life.

They soon discarded teen-age styles in favor of the sophisticated fashions so much more becoming to their tall, willowy figures. They always wore hats and gloves when they went downtown. The family regarded this as evidence of a faint, inherited trace of refinement. They would have been distressed if they had known that the girls were motivated by nothing nobler than a desire to look as grown up as possible.

Whenever the family asked Clementine where the girls spent their afternoons, they received but one answer. "Shopping." They found it hard to understand how the girls could consume so much time spending the few dollars which Edmond sent them each month for clothing and spending money. They had to admit that the girls' costumes evidenced much care and deliberation, but this didn't justify the time they devoted to shopping. They concluded the girls were gratifying their excessive vanity by going around from store to store trying on expensive garments just to admire themselves, without consideration for the salespeople whose time they were wasting.

According to the petition filed in our Court, the girls had gone further than admiring themselves in expensive finery. It was alleged that they were guilty of shoplifting. We looked inquiringly at the store detective who had filed the case. He, too, had been feasting his eyes on the ravishing beauty of the two girls. He stammered as he tried to explain that "it wasn't exactly shoplifting." As a matter of fact, it wasn't shoplifting at all. The girls had never actually "lifted" anything, not even their smallest purchase.

But they had bought hundreds of dollars' worth of clothing and accessories of all kinds, and they had charged them to a fictitious name, which closely resembled one that belonged to a socially prominent family. When the salespersons asked, "Bought by whom?" Stephanie had always answered promptly, "Bought by wife." They avoided the checking which they knew would ensue if they tried to take anything home with them. They had everything they bought delivered to their address, which they had already given the office of the store as the new home address of the account. The fact that the articles were sent also obviated the necessity of their signing anything.

By this simple device, two girls less than sixteen years of age had managed over a period of several months to purchase and receive nearly a thousand dollars' worth of the finest merchandise the store carried. Their purchases appeared on the bill rendered each month to the prominent citizen whose name resembled so nearly the one on their charge slips. Like many other financially independent individuals, he didn't believe in paying his bills too promptly. He put them in the desk for several months before he took them home and asked his wife to check them. She thought that the store bills were always right and that her husband was just trying to make her conscious of how much she spent by asking her to check them. She might have handed them back without looking at them if she hadn't noticed "one dress, $289.00" at the very top of one of the bills. She tried to think which dress that was. She couldn't remember, though she knew she must have bought it. She looked at the date of the purchase. That didn't help her either. She went on looking at other items on the bill to see if she could connect some of them with the dress. Then she looked at the other bills. Finally she handed all of them back to her husband and told him she was sure there were some articles on them she hadn't purchased, but she didn't know which ones they were.

The bills were sent back to the store with a long letter from the prominent citizen, asking for the charge slips on all items appearing thereon. Another month elapsed before anybody in the store got around to figuring out the contents of the letter.

In the meantime, the girls continued buying everything they wanted, and when the prominent citizen received his bill at the end of that month, he promptly brought it home, and his wife promptly declared that she was absolutely certain she hadn't bought a single thing on the bill.

Things began to move more rapidly after that. The store detective discovered that the new home address on the account was not the correct home address of the prominent citizen and that the name on the charge slips was not exactly the same as that of the account. It was very close. The difference could easily have been accounted for as an error on the part of the salesperson, but the name was spelled exactly the same on every charge slip.

The detective called at the address to which the merchandise had been delivered. Clementine answered the door bell and told him that her "young ladies" were still asleep. She couldn't disturb them on any account. He came back in the afternoon only to find them out, but he insisted on waiting. When Clementine left him, he looked around the untidy living room and saw articles which he could identify as having come from his store. When the girls finally came home, however, he was so disarmed by their charm and beauty that he could hardly bring himself to ask them about the merchandise. He pointed to an expensive coat thrown carelessly across the back of one of the chairs and asked if they had purchased it. They said they had, and he asked timidly if they had the charge slip for it. Stephanie said, "Of course not, I bought it three or four months ago." He then began to tell them about the mistake made in charging their purchases to the wrong account. He took out the bills and the charge slips he had brought with him. They admitted having received many of the articles listed, but they denied charging purchases to the prominent citizen. They had charged them to the name on the charge slips, which was slightly different from the name of the prominent citizen. When the detective said that the store had no account in the other name, they laughed and said they had no account either, but he could charge the articles to them if he wanted to.

The store detective took the matter up with his office. He also checked with other large department stores, finding that they, too, had been delivering expensive merchandise to the girls' address. They had charged their purchases to a different account at each store, but in each case they had used a name similar to that of one of the socially prominent customers of the store. Some of these purchases had already been paid for by unsuspecting customers who didn't check their bills.

The District Attorney in the Criminal Court was about to charge the girls with grand larceny on several counts when they produced their birth certificates showing that they were both of Juvenile Court age. The store that had been first to discover the fraud had filed the petition in our Court. Its executives agreed the offense would hardly fall within the legal definition of shoplifting. They were willing to withdraw the petition, or do anything else to cooperate with the Court. None of the other stores filed petitions; they said they would charge these losses up to "education," and they were revising their systems so that no such fraud could be perpetrated upon them again.

We wired the father of the girls. He took a night plane and was in Court the next morning. He was very much ashamed of his daughters' conduct and couldn't understand why they weren't satisfied with the kind of clothes he could afford to give them. He told us about his marriage and the death of his wife and the refusal of the family to have anything to do with Marie and Stephanie. He had thought of remarrying since he had been in New York but doubted that the girls would get along with a stepmother.

He requested us not to contact any members of his family; he feared that if they learned that the older girls were in trouble, it might cause them to "wash their hands" of the three younger children. He thought that he could do more with Marie and Stephanie than anyone else, and he suggested taking them back to New York with him. He was sure the friends with whom he was staying would help him look after the girls.

We talked to the girls a number of times and found that their father was the only person for whom they seemed to have the slightest affection. They felt that they had been "disowned" by their father's family, and as far as they knew, their mother had had no family. It therefore appeared that the plan suggested by their father was the only one which offered any possibilities.

We asked a social agency in New York to investigate the home of Edmond's friends. While we were waiting for the report, we sent the girls to the Guidance Center and also to the Clinic for psychological, psychiatric, and medical check-ups. They were reported to be in good health, above average in intelligence, with no symptoms of psychosis or other mental or emotional disturbances.

Kleptomania, as an explanation for their actions, was ruled out, as the girls had not been motivated by an irresistible impulse to steal. On the contrary, they were in complete possession of themselves at all times. Everything they did was carefully planned. Their purpose was to secure for themselves the expensive clothing and accessories they knew would enhance their beauty and elegance. The scheme they devised accomplished their purpose admirably. Their apparent obliviousness to being found out could be attributed to their youth.

The father returned to the department stores all the articles they could accept, such as jewelry and unworn clothing, and made arrangements to pay for the rest.

Upon receiving a favorable report from New York, we turned the girls over to their father, asking the agency in New York to help him solve their problems. Everything must have gone along fairly well for a while because we received a letter from the agency saying that they saw no further need to service the case and were closing their file.

About three months later the father stopped in to see us. He was in our city on business and wanted to tell us that his original plan hadn't worked out as well as expected because Marie and Stephanie were used to doing just as they pleased without considering the comfort or convenience of anyone else. He had therefore concluded that it was an imposition on his friends to ask them to put up with the girls any longer. He was thinking of taking an apartment when he returned to New York, he said, and he hoped the girls would become interested in keeping house for themselves and for him. We told him we thought they needed some older person with them. We cautioned him against thinking they were as mature as they looked. He said he'd try to arrange for that, too, but he might have to end up by putting them in boarding school.

When we saw him next the housekeeping project had already failed, and the girls had been placed in boarding school. He told us at some length of the events which led up to the boarding school placement.

He had rented a furnished apartment in the same building as the one occupied by his friends. He hadn't expected the girls to be first-class housekeepers because he knew they were naturally lazy and untidy, but they turned out to be even worse than he had anticipated. The apartment was in a state of disorder and confusion at all times, with dirty dishes, soiled clothing, and trash strewn from one end to the other. The father said that the only way he could describe it was to say that it looked like a "bedlam house." Yet the girls themselves always looked immaculate when they went out.

He met them walking along Park Avenue one day, and his artist's eye reveled in the perfection of their beauty. He didn't particularly notice what they were wearing, but with unerring good taste they had selected colors which harmonized with the beautiful tones of their complexions. And their costumes were designed and cut to bring out the perfect lines and symmetry of their forms. He was on his way home when he saw them, and he wondered how many people would believe that these exquisite creatures had emerged from the filth and disorder which greeted his eyes as he entered the apartment.

When they acquired a French poodle, he couldn't understand why they wanted a dog because they had never been fond of pets. But when he saw that the little tufts of hair on the dog's body were being dyed to match or complement some of their costumes, he realized that they regarded the poodle as just another adjunct to the adornment of their persons.

Having had no experience in purchasing fancy dogs, he had no idea that the poodle was worth twelve hundred dollars. Nor did he suspect that the cost of grooming such a dog ran well over fifty dollars a month.

Although he provided the girls with a liberal allowance for clothing, he lacked the discernment which would have enabled him to see that the expensive outfits in which they were appearing could not be purchased with the kind of money he was giving them.

Things went along this way for several months. No one can tell how much longer they might have been able to continue if Stephanie hadn't conceived the idea that she should have a mink coat. The saleswoman in one of the stores where she had been looking at dresses induced her to try on a new model and went into ecstasies over how well it looked on Stephanie. She incited the same admiration in all the other shops in which she tried on mink coats. The store people had seen professional models who could wear mink like that, but a customer, never!

Since they had come to New York, the girls had been
making their purchases in the small, exclusive shops
where the profits were so large that every precaution was
taken to avoid offending customers. But in her quest
for the mink coat most becoming to her, Stephanie saw
one she liked in the show window of one of the "big"
stores. When she tried it on, Marie agreed that it suited
her better than any of the others. She went back to some
of the little shops and described it, and when they could
show her nothing like it, they offered to have one made
for her. She thought this was "too risky," and so she
studied the *Social Register* and the society columns of the
newspapers, using more care than usual in working out
the fictitious name which she would use in the big store.
Then she went to the office and had no difficulty in having
the home address of the account changed because she
looked more like a wealthy and socially prominent young
matron than any of those who actually enjoyed this status.

Then she went back to the saleswoman who had shown
her the coat she had set her heart on. She asked to try
it on again. She pretended to be hesitant and unde-
cided, letting the saleswoman think that she had persuaded her to make the purchase. When it was discovered that there was a slight discrepancy between the
name appearing on the charge slip and the one in which
the account stood, the saleswoman confessed she had
been so excited about making the sale that she could
easily have made an error in spelling. She corrected the
slip, and the coat was delivered the next morning.

Stephanie avoided wearing the coat at times when
her father might see her. Fully appreciating his obtuse-
ness in matters of women's clothes and doubting his
ability to recognize genuine mink when he saw it, she

nevertheless knew him to share the ridiculous idea, common to most men, that all fur coats are expensive. When a young man called at the apartment during the girls' absence and asked their father if a mink coat had been delivered there, he answered, "No." He was sure he would have remembered it if he had seen a fur coat on either of his daughters. He also answered, "No," when the man inquired if anyone with the name appearing on the charge slip resided in the apartment. He said he guessed his mind must not have functioned properly because he didn't even suspect what had happened until Stephanie walked in wearing the mink coat.

The father was overwhelmed with astonishment when he learned that his daughters had obtained thousands of dollars' worth of expensive merchandise since they had come to New York by using fictitious names resembling those of established charge accounts.

He explained his failure to anticipate and guard against a repetition of what had occurred in New Orleans by the fact that he regarded New York merchants as keen, hard-headed businessmen, whom he would never have believed gullible enough to be taken in by two teen-age girls. He himself had found it impossible to get credit when he first went to New York, even though he held a responsible position and had good references.

The mink coat was still just as good as when it was purchased, and the store willingly took it back. The French poodle was also returned to the pet shop. But Stephanie's father had to borrow half a year's salary from his firm to pay for the other articles the girls had bought.

Marie and Stephanie were still of Juvenile Court age under the laws of New York. After considering the complaints filed by several of the stores, as well as other ele-

ments in the case, the Court placed them on probation
in the custody of their father. But the Court knew of
the father's previous unsuccessful attempts to supervise
his daughters, and it was therefore made a condition of
the probation that the girls be placed in boarding school
and kept there until further orders of the Court.

A few months after this, the father telephoned us from
New York to ask if we had seen anything of the girls.
They had run away from the boarding school. He
thought it just possible that they might have returned to
our city. He had already been in contact with his family,
although he thought it unlikely that the girls would get
in touch with them. We promised to make inquiries
and be on the lookout for the girls and notify the father
if we discovered any clues to their whereabouts.

The Bureau of Missing Persons wired a description of
the girls to every large city in the country, and the father
spared no trouble or expense in his attempt to locate his
daughters. It seemed impossible that two girls, as unusual in appearance as they were, could long continue
to escape detection. But the search remained fruitless
for more than three months. The father never gave up
or diminished his efforts to find them until he learned
of their tragic fate.

Even after we found that Marie and Stephanie had
headed for California when they left the boarding school
in New York, we were still unable to trace the zig-zag
route they had taken in order to throw their pursuers off
their track. They were first seen in San Francisco more
than a month after the date of their disappearance from
the boarding school. None of those who saw them suspected the two beautiful ladies of being runaway school
girls. They apparently tried to carry on in their usual

fashion for a while, without being as successful as they had been in New York and New Orleans.

Their clothes were rather shabby when they arrived in San Francisco, and whether for this reason or some other, their attempts to charge expensive purchases to fictitious accounts failed in most instances.

They seemed to drop out of sight for a while. When next seen they were living in Chinatown. This time they were handsomely and expensively dressed; the costumes and jewels and furs which they wore came from the finest shops of the city. Investigation revealed that they charged their purchases to the account of a wealthy Chinaman, whose name was correctly spelled on the charge slips and whose address was the same as theirs. But whether the purchases were made with or without the knowledge and consent of the Chinaman will never be known. When the Chinaman was found, he had plunged into his own heart the knife with which he had killed the two girls.

For some unaccountable reason the story received little publicity. It never appeared in our local papers. This was fortunate for the three little sisters, who are still living here and who are a source of pride and joy to the relatives who befriended them.

The father blames himself for what happened; yet when he looks back, it appears that any point at which he might have chosen a different course than the one he followed was already too late. When he asked us whether we thought the tragic end of the older girls might have been averted if they had been accepted by the family as their younger sisters were, we humbly confessed that we didn't know the answer. It would have been no answer to tell him that the disastrous mistake was made when he married a girl whom he must have known would not be acceptable to his family. It would have been begging the question to have told him that his beautiful daughters would have presented no problems if they had never been born.

13

FOSTER HOME

It has been said that the human heart loves to associate itself with some dear spot which it calls home. Those who have dealt with children know they love the home they regard as theirs, regardless of what it is like.

This may be one reason why institutions for children are now designated "homes" instead of "orphan asylums." Whatever the reason, we think it well the name has been changed, not only because of the tragic implications of the former designation, but also because these institutions now include few orphans among their population. Most are now so overcrowded with the children of divorced or separated parents that when courts seek to place a genuine orphan in one, they are usually met with a regretful "No Vacancy."

When every adoption agency has a long list of approved applicants waiting impatiently to give children homes, it is difficult for the public to understand why all these charitable institutions for children are filled to overflowing. The explanation is simple. Almost none of the children in our charitable institutions are available for adoption because most have living parents who refuse to give them up.

The public is also somewhat confused in its thinking about foster homes. Many people regard adoptive homes and foster homes as the same. We are always careful to explain the difference to parents when suggesting their children be placed in foster homes.

Theoretically and ideally, the foster home is the nearest substitute for the child's own home which has yet been found. But we should never forget that it is at best a substitute. This is the inevitable result of the fact that foster home placements are temporary placements, even though children often remain in them for many years.

In order to meet standard requirements, the income in the foster home must be adequate to support the home, without considering amounts received for board and expenses of children placed there. The rates paid for board vary with different public and private agencies. In some cases extra allowances are available for clothing, medical, and miscellaneous expenses. Ample living and play space must be provided for the children; good, nourishing, well-balanced meals must be supplied. Although special diets are sometimes necessary, it is not desirable for the foster home children to be served their meals separately from the rest of the family; participation in all family gatherings is considered an important factor in orientation to the life of the home.

The ideal foster home is one in which the father and mother are well-adjusted individuals, with no emotional or health problems of their own, and with a comfortable, roomy house they are willing to share with children who have lost their own homes. The foster mother must not be employed outside the home. She should be a warm-hearted, outgoing person who will give her foster children the love and affection more important to a child than either food or raiment.

But while she is expected to display all those virtues which we commonly associate with natural motherhood, the foster mother must be able to give up her foster children willingly and cheerfully, at a moment's notice, whenever their own parents can provide a suitable home for them or when some other plan is made for them by the agency which places them. Unlike adopted children, foster children can never belong to their foster parents. Even in those cases where the children become available for adoption, the foster parents are not eligible to apply for them.

The foster child must be made to feel that he belongs in the foster home, but the foster parents must never acquire a possessive attitude toward him. They must take him in, making him believe that he is loved and wanted as a member of the family circle, but when it is time for him to go, they must remember that he was only a visitor in their home. It is part of their undertaking that they will give generously of themselves, expecting nothing in return other than the satisfaction of knowing they have temporarily filled a gap in the life of a child.

If this were more widely known, it would be easier for people to understand why there is always a scarcity of good foster homes and why some used fall far short of the ideal. Courts which deal with children are well aware of these facts. They have to learn not to be too critical of foster homes in which public and private agencies place the wards of the court.

Even so, we never considered a bad foster home better than a good institution. We knew opportunities for prolonged mistreatment of a child without detection are far greater in a foster home than in any institution. This might not be so if foster homes could be carefully and closely supervised, but this is seldom possible in actual practice. Agency workers usually notify foster homes in advance of their visits, as they do not wish to be thought of as spies or snoopers. They usually see only what the foster parents intend them to see, and they too often don't see even that as case loads are too heavy to permit frequent visits.

All this is by way of explanation of our choice of the tragic story of Mona, a pitiful little child who was placed in a bad foster home, rather than the happy experience of some more fortunate child who was placed with one of those ideal foster mothers who should be regarded as among God's noblest creatures.

The details of this case stand out in our mind the more clearly because Mona was one of the first children to be brought before us the day we took office as Judge of the Juvenile Court. The fact that we had formerly served on the Board of the Agency which had made the foster home placement and that we knew it to be one of the best child welfare agencies in the South no doubt contributed to the impact of this case on the mind of the Court.

Mona was a child who was not available for adoption, but the agency had reason to believe that she was going to require "long time placement." They could have tried to transfer her to some other agency for institutional placement, but the Guidance Center's report indicated Mona needed things no institution could provide. Although only four years old, she craved affection and appreciation, and she was almost painfully shy in the presence of other children.

When examined at the Clinic, she was found to be underweight, and a special diet was prescribed for her. It was also recommended that she be exposed to as much fresh air and sunshine as possible. An institution was contra-indicated, even if the agency could find one which would accept the child.

The agency had one foster home, located on the outskirts of the city, that had been investigated and approved but never used. It was in a suburb which had been so slow in building up that it was almost like the country. There were several large open lots between the foster home and the house of the nearest neighbor, but it never occurred to the agency worker that the absence of close neighbors would be a disadvantage. On the contrary, she was delighted to find the child would have all the intervening space in which to play.

She had complete confidence in the foster mother with whom she placed Mona. During the three years that Mona lived in the home nothing had happened to cause her to lose this confidence. She visited the home once a month during the first year of the placement and once every three or four months during the succeeding years. Mona had ample opportunity to complain to the visitor if she had wished to do so, but she was a naturally timid child, and she had probably been made more so by the mistreatment she received at the hands of her foster mother.

When the child was six years old, the visitor suggested that it was time for Mona to go to school. She didn't think to ask to see Mona's report cards, however, when the foster mother said she was attending the public school and doing well. Afterwards it was discovered that these report cards revealed many long, unexplained absences from school.

Even when the child was brought into Court, bearing unmistakable evidence of the foster mother's cruelty, the visitor could not think of a single incident or circumstance that should have suggested to her that something was wrong, unless it was the fact that other workers for the same agency had repeatedly turned down this foster home when they had children to place. The visitor knew this because she was eager for Mona to have some playmates when she found that there were no other children in the neighborhood. But the other workers could give no good reasons for not using this foster home other than an inexplicable dislike they had conceived for the foster mother and which they attributed to intuition when they learned about what had happened to Mona.

According to the agency's records, Mona was seven years old a few days before we saw her for the first time. She was no larger than the average child of five, and she walked with the short steps of an even smaller child, but her face looked like that of a little old woman. The visitor removed the single garment which the child was wearing, and we saw that her entire body was covered with bruises of varying shades of black and purple. The skin was broken in many places, and blood was oozing from the deep new cuts as well as from some of the older scars. Her wrists and ankles were circled by bands of raw flesh, from which all of the skin had been torn. There wasn't an inch of the child's back or buttocks which could be touched even lightly without causing her excruciating pain.

The District Attorney asked Mona how long the beatings had been going on and when they had commenced, but her answer to every question was, "I can't remember." No one will ever know how long that child had been subjected to indescribable torture. Nor can anyone say how much longer it might have continued if it had not been for two workmen who heard her cries and went to her assistance.

They were carpenters who had gone to work early that morning in order to lay out the lines for a house to be built on one of the lots adjoining the foster home. They were looking for the surveyor's stakes and taking measurements, thinking what a "nice, quiet neighborhood" it was, when they heard a piercing scream. They thought it sounded like a child, and they stopped to determine where it came from. In a few moments there was another piteous cry, and then another and another in quick succession. The workmen quickly crossed over to the house and climbed up to one of the side windows. They looked in and were horrified at what they saw.

A child was tied face downward on a bed. A woman was standing over it, beating it furiously with a whip. Each time the woman brandished the lash and brought it down with a crackling sound, a blood-curdling cry rent the air, and the child's body writhed in agony. The woman's face was turned away from the window, but the men could see that her body was convulsed at each stroke of the whip as though she too felt the cut of the lash.

She was apparently oblivious to everything else about her, and she gave no sign of having heard the men when they broke through the window and called to her to stop. But when they tried to wrench the whip from her grasp, she fought them with the strength and ferocity of a maniac. When they succeeded in getting it away from her, they locked her in an adjoining room and cut the ropes binding the child to the bed. They waited until the child painfully drew on a dress which had been lying on the floor beside the bed. They wanted to carry her to their truck, but they could find no way to lift her without hurting her.

They asked her if the woman was her mother, and when she answered, "No," they asked her a number of other questions. She could tell them very little, but she did know the name of her visitor. The workmen led her out of the house, trying not to touch the little wrists, which were raw and bleeding where they had been burned by the ropes. They made a pallet so that she could lie face downward in the truck. They drove slowly and carefully, but at the slightest jolt of the vehicle, she cried out in pain. When they arrived at the visitor's home, she asked them to bring the child to the Court.

The sight of the child's condition was indeed a "baptism of fire" for us. We had never dreamed that any human being could be guilty of such brutality toward a child, and we were further saddened by evidence of the fact that the cruel mistreatment must have been going on for a long time. We could also see that the child's spirit had been broken, for she cringed in fright whenever a word or question was addressed to her.

The foster mother was arrested, and our District Attorney referred the case against her to the Criminal Court, where a lunacy commission pronounced her insane. She was committed to the State Hospital, where she is still confined in the ward for the criminally insane.

We sent Mona to a hospital, but it was many months before the bruises and abrasions on her poor little body cleared up and healed. And it was a matter of years before we could overcome the fearfulness and apprehension which had taken possession of the child. She fled in panic at the approach of a stranger. The slightest unexpected gesture would cause her to shrink in fear of an anticipated blow. She often ran away and hid when she became frightened, and it was sometimes many hours before she could be found. She stole things she could have had for the asking, and she lied when there was no occasion to do so. She continued to walk with the short little steps which we had noticed when she was first brought to the Court and for which no explanation could be found except that she still regarded herself as a much smaller child than she actually was.

Mona had many problems, but all of them were gradually overcome. She has developed into a happy, healthy child, and although she has lost all her former innate fear and timidity, she has retained a certain shyness of manner which is very appealing and has won for her many good friends.

Her rehabilitation was a slow, painful process. It never could have been accomplished if it had not been for the almost superhuman patience and the untiring devotion of one of those good foster mothers for whom we are sure there will be reserved a special place in Heaven.

14

WAR BABY

The day of the week given over to adoptions in our Court was usually the brightest on our calendar. It was heartwarming to see the adoptive parents so eager to give their love and faith and all their worldly possessions to children who were as yet almost strangers to them. It is said that "all the world loves a lover"; but we have often thought that the world should love adoptive parents equally well. They set for all of us an example of love that is truly selfless and that never falters under the most trying circumstances. The love of natural parents for their children is easily understandable; it partakes of their love of themselves. Just as most human beings experience no great difficulty in continuing to love themselves, in spite of their numerous faults and failings, so natural parents find it easy to tolerate shortcomings of children who are "flesh of their flesh." But adoptive parents, who take "other people's children" into their lives and their hearts, must bear with vicissitudes that are an indispensable part of childhood and adolescence and the process of growing up, without the compensating gratification of self-love.

263

A natural mother's love for her child is sometimes thought to derive from the pain and suffering in which she brings him into the world. But let no one think that adoptive parents receive children without difficulty. First, they have to find an agency which places children with people of their race, color, and religion. If they succeed in getting over these initial hurdles, they are permitted to file an application, but they are usually told that there are many hundreds—in some cases, thousands— of applications that will have precedence over theirs. If they refuse to be discouraged, they can supply the answers to long pages of questions and also tell "in their own words" why they want to adopt a baby. If they have expressed preference about age and sex, they are asked to explain the reason for their preference. They are also required to give detailed information as to their immediate and remote forebears, as well as much other information that often does not seem pertinent to the question of their fitness to adopt a child.

If they remain undeterred by this "red tape" and have not disqualified themselves by their answers to the questionnaire, they may look forward to an interview—regarded by many adoptive parents as the "oral examination" which they must pass. An agency worker comes to the home of the adoptive parents for the initial interview; subsequent interviews usually take place in the office of the agency.

When information indicates that adoptive parents meet the requirements of the agency, their statements are verified by checking public records. Careful investigation is made of everything that might possibly affect the suitability of the applicants to become adoptive parents.

If all this results in the approval of the application, applicants are notified that they have been placed on "the list." The length of time they will have to wait for a child depends upon many unpredictable factors. It is usually longer for those who specify the age and sex of the child they wish to adopt. Long waiting periods must also be expected by applicants with traits and backgrounds not ordinarily found in children available for adoption, for there is a studied attempt to match the child with the adoptive parents.

When we consider the care exercised in selecting adoptive homes, it is small wonder that the temporary decrees, rendered by the Court when children are placed for adoption, are nearly always followed in due course by final judgments giving the child into the permanent care and custody of the adoptive parents—to the same extent as if it had been born to them.

But the case of Jerry Jones had been exceptional from the very beginning. We were not surprised when the Welfare Department reported that they were unable to recommend a final judgment at the expiration of a year from the date of the temporary decree. The child had failed to adjust in the adoptive home. At the urgent request of the adoptive parents, the Department consented to extend supervision for another year. The child was still quite young; it was possible that he might ultimately respond to the loving care and devotion of his adoptive parents. The Court therefore ordered the case to be continued and to be reassigned. The Welfare Department put a special worker on the case, hoping her training and experience might help the adoptive parents in the difficult task they had undertaken.

The adoptive parents cooperated with the case worker, as well as with the Guidance Center and the Clinic, and exhibited almost superhuman patience in endeavoring to carry out every suggestion that was made. Jerry was nearly three years old when he was placed. Though now four, he was still too young to understand the meaning of the word "cooperation." But it was evident that he did understand how to resist everything that anyone tried to do for him.

When his adoptive mother invited neighborhood children to play with him, he went inside the house, refusing to come out of his hiding place until the children left. When he was sent to nursery school, not only would he have nothing to do with other children, but he hit them and broke their toys if they came near him. The teacher tried letting him alone, ignoring his objectionable behavior. She also tried giving him special attention. She was confident that he would ultimately respond to her efforts, but she finally gave up when he became "absolutely impossible."

The adoptive parents were not discouraged even when they tried placing him in kindergarten and several small schools with no better success. They thought he still had "lots of time" before he reached school age, and they decided to keep him at home and not try to force on him the companionship of other children. The adoptive mother tried to interest him in planting a little garden and doing other things with her, and the father devised games to play with him. But Jerry continued to reject them and everything they offered.

He ate only what he pleased. If something he didn't like was put on his plate, he threw it on the floor. He was losing weight steadily, but the doctor could find nothing organically wrong with him and declared that he thought that the child was "possessed of the imp of the perverse." He had been the family doctor of the adoptive parents for many years, and he regarded Jerry as undeserving of all the love and devotion which was being lavished on him. This was also the opinion of some of the neighbors, whom Jerry must have heard talking one evening. He got up early the next morning and smeared their freshly painted houses with black roofing tar.

The adoptive parents were much concerned over Jerry's refusal to use the word "our" in referring to their car, their home, and all the other things which they were willing to share with him. Even though they addressed each other as "Mama" and "Papa" for Jerry's benefit, he continued to call them "Mabel" and "Bert."

In spite of all this, they loved the child and they were determined not to give him up. But in the end they had to. Jerry ate less and less. He finally refused to eat anything at all. The doctor said there was nothing the matter with him, "just stubbornness." When he stopped talking and they thought he had lost his voice, the doctor said the same thing, "just stubbornness." The adoptive parents were now convinced that if the child was so unhappy with them that he would neither eat nor speak, it was time to let him go.

Even as they agreed to give him up, they wanted assurance that he wouldn't be placed where he would be mistreated in any way. They feared that his exasperating behavior might make it hard for anyone else to love him as much as they did.

We knew one person who would love him in spite of everything, and we knew that Jerry would love her too, but we didn't know if we should tell her about the child. We believed that time might have healed somewhat the wounds which she inflicted upon herself when she parted with him, and we hesitated to reopen those wounds and prod them again into sharp pain unless there was some reasonable hope that it could help Jerry. We knew we had to do it when Jerry became so weak that he had to be taken to the hospital for intravenous feeding, and the doctor reported that they had to bind his hands and arms to keep him from pushing away the tube.

For almost two years he had fought us, and we could see that he was going to fight until the very end. It was obvious that Jerry wanted something, and though he didn't know what it was, he felt that we were keeping it from him. He had done everything that a child could do to show us that nothing we had offered him filled his need. Though he had never asked for his mother or his sisters and had probably forgotten them, we knew he wanted them and that he could accept no substitutes. He had been provided with an excellent adoptive home where he was surrounded by love and affection, but he was like a man starving to death with a luscious banquet spread out in front of him. We knew of one morsel that would restore him in body and spirit if he could partake of it. We had to try to get it for him, even at the risk of snatching it away from others who might also be sorely in need of it.

We have often marveled at the strength of the tie which binds all children to their natural parents. We say "all children" advisedly, for we have observed it to be universal. We've heard both children and parents vehemently deny the existence of the bond, but subsequent events have always proved that there was no truth in these denials. The tie exists between good children and bad parents, as well as between bad children and good parents, and we have come to believe that it is al-

most indestructible. When souls are bared and emotions
unrestrained, as they so often are in a court like ours,
you see clearly into human hearts and minds, and you
are sometimes given the light to understand what you see
there.

Jerry's mother responded promptly to our summons,
and we could see that she was excited and upset when
she came in. Her first words showed that she intuitively
knew what we dreaded to tell her. "Something's happened to my boy, and I'm to blame. I promised I would
never see him again, but now I must."

We knew about the promise and about all that had
gone before it.

Nearly two years before Jerry's birth, his mother's husband had been called into the armed services and had
been assigned to duty in the Far East. His mother had
three adorable little girls, who should have been sufficient
to keep her from becoming unbearably lonely during the
long absence of their father. But they were all too young
to understand how she felt, the eldest being but seven
at the time. The mother was young and attractive and
filled to overflowing with the joy of living. She missed
her husband terribly, and she also missed the gay circle
of friends in which she no longer felt welcome after her
husband's departure. She was the odd woman who cre-
ates a problem for a hostess at any time, but particularly
in wartime when men are all too scarce anyway.

She had been waiting impatiently for her husband's
return when she met a handsome young officer who was
in our city awaiting orders which would send him overseas. She saw at once that he was attracted to her, and
she welcomed the diversion which his attentions offered.
She was never in love with him, nor he with her, but they

each found in the other the gay and charming companionship which could make the months pass quickly while they were waiting.

Time and proximity did the rest, and neither of them blamed the other for what happened. The officer received his sailing orders and left without knowing that Jerry's mother was pregnant. She saw no point in writing him about it. She was glad that she hadn't when she learned that he had been killed in the Battle of the Bulge two days before Jerry was born.

Relatives, friends, and neighbors checked with each other to be sure that they were right about the husband's continuous absence for nearly two years prior to Jerry's birth. Then they counted on their fingers and shook their heads ominously as they waited for the husband's return.

Jerry's mother waited too, and during all the time she waited, she cherished her baby with a love far greater than any she had known for her other children. Was it because he was her only son, or was she trying to make up to him for having brought him into a world which would call him "bastard"?

She performed all her household tasks with Jerry in her arms, and she never put him down unless it was absolutely necessary. She talked to him and cooed at him and deluded herself into thinking that he understood her when he returned her smiles.

She had few visitors in these days except those who came to tell her what that mysterious entity, commonly referred to as "they," was saying about her. Her in-laws stayed away from her entirely and stopped inviting the little girls to spend week ends with them. She had always let them have the children, even during those first dark days after her husband's departure when she needed to fill the great gap left in her life by his absence. She knew that her husband's parents sadly missed their son and that having his children with them helped to ease the aching of their lonely hearts. But they couldn't forget that the children were hers, too, and the very sight of them now reminded their grandparents of the disgrace which the children's mother had brought upon their son.

She was thankful no word had reached her husband. She could tell that by his letters in which he said that the thought of her was all that had kept him alive when he was captured and forced to march through the steaming jungles of the Pacific Islands. He remained a prisoner of war for many months and spent many more months in an overseas hospital after he was freed. His return was delayed several times. His wife shared his bitter disappointment each time his return was delayed, and they both prayed earnestly to be reunited.

She had almost given up expecting him when he finally arrived late one evening without any notice to prepare her for his coming. She had already put Jerry to bed, and she looked up from the small garment she was mending and saw her husband standing before her. His face was drawn and colorless, and he looked almost cadaverous to the wife who had not seen him in four years. She knew he must have suffered far more than he had let her know, for he looked ten years older than when he had left. Her heart went out to him in love and pity.

He didn't want to talk about the war, or what he had been through since he last saw her. "That's over and done with. I'm back with you, my darling, and that's all that matters." Nor would he let her call the children or go to the kitchen to get something for him to eat. He held her by both hands and devoured her with his eyes. He told her that he hadn't looked at another woman since he left her, and she knew that he spoke the truth, for he had always held their marriage to be sacred and blessed. Then he drew her into his arms and kissed her face and eyes and hair as he told her that the joy of coming home to her made up for everything that he had suffered.

She tried to free herself from his embrace. "I have something to tell you," she began. But he kissed the next words from her lips. "Tell me how much you love me. That's all I want to hear." It was taking more courage than she had expected, but she knew she had to do it some time, and she began once more. "I do love you with all my heart, but I don't know if you'll believe it when you hear what I have to tell you." He would have stopped her again, but she forced him to listen.

She spoke plainly, relating the facts just as they had occurred, without any attempt to escape the blame for what had happened. She spared herself nothing and admitted that she didn't even have the excuse of having been in love with the young officer. She humbly expressed her admiration for the strength of character which had enabled her husband to keep faith with her through all that he had endured; but she told him that she would have understood and forgiven him if he had given way to weakness and temptation. She hoped he would be able to forgive her, and she would do everything she could to make it up to him.

When she could think of nothing more to say, she looked at her husband and saw that he was staring at her incredulously. His gaunt body was in violent convulsions. He tried to say something, but his chattering teeth prevented his lips from forming the words. She put her cool hand on his forehead which was unnaturally hot. He was shaking with cold and burning with fever at the same time. She wrapped him in a blanket and gave him a warm drink, and he was too weak to resist her as she drew his head to her bosom and talked to him soothingly as though he were a sick child. "You poor darling, you never told me you had the jungle fever. But you'll get well, now that you're home and have your wife to nurse you."

When the chill had passed, he was still pathetically weak. He put his head on the table and sobbed piteously. His little girls came in from their play and tried to kiss him, but his grief had taken possession of him. He was still weeping audibly when his wife left him to give the little girls their supper and put them to bed. When she returned to the living room, he had gone.

He returned the next morning, looking more haggard and worn than when he had arrived. He said he had been walking all night, trying to think. He washed his face and hands and, after drinking some coffee, left again, saying that he was going to his parents.

It was three days before his wife saw him again. He came to her then and told her that he had made up his mind. He would forgive her and try to forget what had happened, but she couldn't keep the boy because he would be a constant reminder of "the other man." He said he already hated the child intensely, although he had learned of his existence only a few days previously and had never seen him. She looked at him unbelievingly, asking him what he meant. He said that she would have to give up the boy.

She was willing to do anything to atone for the great wrong she had thoughtlessly committed against her husband. But the child! Surely he had done nothing to merit such cruel treatment. She thought it over for a few moments and then told her husband she couldn't make an innocent child suffer for her sin. He said that if she refused his offer, there was only one alternative. He would have to divorce her, and in order to get custody of his three little girls, he would have to allege adultery.

It was a bitter choice for a mother to have to make. There was her fatherless child, to whom she had done a grave injustice by bringing him into such a heartless world. There was the husband whom she had never ceased to love, now sick and needing her care, to whom she had likewise done an injustice. There were also the three little daughters, who would have to bear the brunt of the scandal if their mother were branded an adulteress. She loved all her children equally, and she tried to decide which of them needed her the most. The boy was so young that he could probably forget her very quickly. She had often heard that a merciful Providence gives children short memories. The girls were older and, because they were girls, they would perhaps need a mother's care and guidance more than the boy would.

It was hard for her to think of Jerry in any place except her arms, but she forced herself to consider what would be best for him if she decided to give him up. She knew that children in institutions missed almost everything that makes a child's life worthwhile, but she had never seen an adopted child not loved and cherished by its adoptive parents. She told her husband that "if" she decided to part with Jerry, she would want him to be adopted. This was satisfactory to him, but she had to promise to give him up completely and never see him again. She wasn't sure she could live up to such a promise, but the worker from the adoption agency told her that she would have no choice. If she surrendered Jerry for adoption, she would never know who his adoptive parents were, nor would they know who she was.

She asked her husband to give her a week to think it over. He stayed with his parents until the week was up, and then he came for her answer. She would have pleaded for more time, but she could see the strain was telling on him; and every day that she was with Jerry was making it harder for her to give him up. She agreed to her husband's terms. They came into Court together to surrender the child.

We talked to each of them separately. Then we went over the whole matter with both of them in one last effort to dissuade them. The husband's jaw was set. His was the only dry eye in the room as this weeping mother offered up her child in sacrifice for her sin. We waited in vain for some miracle, but no angel appeared with a substitute for the sacrifice of the boy. The gods of propriety were less merciful than Abraham's God. The mother submitted to her husband's will.

We knew what she must have suffered in giving up her child and in learning to live with her remorse in the days that followed. She nursed her husband back to health, and he was apparently just as devoted to her as he had ever been. He seemed to have wholly forgiven her, but she couldn't forgive herself. She knew neither happiness nor peace of mind; the thought of her child gnawed constantly at her heart and conscience.

Now we had to tell her that her boy was dying, and we didn't know of anyone who could save him unless she could.

It was nearly two years since Jerry had seen her; but when she went to the hospital and leaned over his bed, he opened his eyes, and the lips which had been so long silent murmured, "Mama." She gently released the bandages which were binding his arms, and she took one of his thin little hands in hers and kissed it. She sat by his bed all that night and all the next day and the next night. During all this time, he did not once try to push away the tube which was bringing nourishment to his wasted body. Nor did he fight any of the nurses or internes who came to minister to him. His condition improved so rapidly that the doctors said it "was nothing short of miraculous."

And so Jerry was saved by a miracle, after all.

When he was discharged from the hospital, his mother took him home with her. She told her husband that he could get a divorce, and he did. But he couldn't get it on grounds of adultery because he had condoned "the offense against his honor" by living with her after he knew about it; he was therefore unable to take her little girls away from her. It was also too late for him to institute legal proceedings to deny that he was the father of Jerry.

We hear from Jerry's mother occasionally, and while it hasn't been easy for her to bring up four children without a father, she is living happily with her little brood. Jerry has adjusted well and his bright, sunny disposition has been a joy to his mother. She no longer has any feelings of guilt about him. Perhaps we were wrong when we tried to stay her husband's hand as he lifted the sacrificial knife and plunged it into her heart. Perhaps there was no other way in which she could have found peace and happiness.

EPILOGUE

The stories of these cases have given a picture of the kinds of children who appear before juvenile courts, the troubles in which they become entangled, and something of the means a court has at its disposal to help them. Inevitably the question arises, "What is the status of preventive justice today?"

A little more than fifty years ago we established juvenile courts. These courts were founded on the conviction that it is far better to rescue young lives and prevent crime than to punish criminals after crime has been committed. All forty-eight of our states now have juvenile courts; there are now more than three thousand of these courts in the country.

The new idea of justice which these courts were set up to administer was a complete departure from the old idea, which was based upon vengeance and retribution and strove to fit the punishment to the crime. Punitive justice is exemplified in the representations of the goddess of justice depicted as a woman with her eyes blindfolded and with nicely balanced scales in one hand and a sword in the other. One side of the scales is for crime, and the other is for punishment; when they balance, justice is done. The sword is placed in her hand to signify her ability to enforce her decrees.

277

Our new idea of justice must tear the bandage from her eyes so that she can see each individual child as he stands before her and learn everything that she can about him—how he came to be what he is, what is wrong in his life, what deprivations and failures and frustrations he has suffered. Justice can throw away the scales and the sword, for there is no punishment to be weighed and no need for show of power or authority in dealing with children; she will need both her hands, as well as her head and her heart, to lead the child from the darkness of delinquency to the light of hope and promise.

When the juvenile court was established to administer this new type of justice, there was no charted course it could follow, no body of rules or precedents on which decisions could be based. The idea has been sound because it is still alive after having weathered periodic "crime waves," followed first by hysterical public indignation and then by disheartening apathy and indifference. No one ever seriously suggested abandoning our new justice which has saved so many children; but there is a tendency to let it become obsolete.

This is all the more regrettable when we realize that in dealing with children time is of the essence. A week, a month, a year are all short intervals in the life of an adult, but to a child they are an eternity. It is always later than we think when a child is brought into court. Forces have been at work affecting personality and character and influencing behavior patterns of delinquents long before they come into conflict with the law. A child's development never stands still; for better or for worse, it proceeds at a very rapid pace; any delay in diagnosing his trouble or in administering treatment may prove disastrous.

After having traveled extensively in this country and abroad and having visited juvenile courts and their auxiliary facilities wherever I went, I failed to find a single court which was equipped with staff and facilities adequate to accomplish the best possible results. A few communities have adequate buildings for their courts. A few others may have newly constructed detention homes. But by and large there is an appalling lack of the essential requirements for bringing these courts up to standard.

The greatest need of most courts is an adequate number of probation officers qualified by training, experience, and temperament to perform the difficult task of re-forming the attitudes and character of maladjusted youth. This has resulted in an ever-widening gap between the theory and the practice of probation. Although, theoretically, probation is still the best method yet devised for dealing with delinquency, probation as actually practiced often amounts to little more than a routine of perfunctory office visits, with none of that individualized treatment essential for effective probation work.

What has been said of the wide gap between the theory and practice of probation is also true of foster home programs. According to a report of the United States Children's Bureau, foster home programs have "bogged down" all over the country, and there is a proportionately larger number of delinquents among children brought up in foster homes than among those who have grown up in orphanages and other such institutions. But the good foster home is still regarded as the best substitute which has yet been found for a child's own home, and the failure of these programs must be due to the substandard homes used because suitable homes were unavailable.

Although it may not be practical at this time to provide every court with a staff of physicians, psychiatrists, psychologists, and social scientists, there is no good reason why some plan cannot be worked out to make the services of such experts available to the courts on a regional, district, or other basis.

The same is true of institutions. Although authorities are in agreement that institutional placement should be regarded as a last resort, there are cases in which there is no alternative to such placement. The courts should have available institutions designed and maintained to meet the various needs of children in the condition in which the courts find them. But it is a well-known fact that there are few correctional institutions in the entire country which are equipped to give their inmates anything more than custodial care. Courts are ever conscious of the fact that sooner or later every child committed to an institution must be returned to society. It cannot be denied that the youth comes out of the average reform school far better versed in the ways of crime than when he went in.

The task of the judge has been likened to that of the physician. In many important respects it is, because the court must first diagnose and then treat the individual child, just as the doctor must first find out what is wrong with each patient and then prescribe the appropriate remedy. But there is this difference: certain types of cases should be hospitalized and no harm will result to the patient even if it should subsequently appear that hospitalization was unnecessary. But it cannot be said that it will do no harm to institutionalize a child unnecessarily, or that it is always safe to permit a child with serious behavior problems to remain at large.

Most courts understandably prefer to try probation even though the chances of success in this type of treatment are limited by the lack of properly qualified probation officers. The court may decide to place the child on probation either in his own home or in a foster home. Permitting the child to remain in his own home is preferable wherever possible, because it is always doubtful that there is anything we can do for a child which will make up to him for the injury we inflict when we sever the vital ties that bind him to his home. But when all attempts to rehabilitate the child in his own home meet with failure, probation in a foster home may still have a better chance of success than confinement in a repressive, regimented type of institution.

Regardless of what plan may be made for the child, the court must always work with parents. All too often these parents are inadequate and irresponsible, but it would be a serious mistake for the court to ignore them or underestimate their importance in the life of the child. Frequently they have failed the child in many important respects, but their cooperation is usually essential for the success of the court's efforts on the child's behalf.

The suggestion of punishment of parents for the delinquency of their children is one that recurs at intervals. The proponents of such punishment point to China and other Asiatic countries where such measures are said to be effective in producing good children. The statutes of most of our states do provide for the punishment of adults for contributing to the delinquency of children. It is under these statutes that some courts were prevailed upon to sentence parents to attendance at "Parental Schools" as a penalty for the delinquency of their children. But inadequate and misguided though they may be, most

parents of delinquents are well-meaning and could not
be justly convicted of intentionally contributing to their
children's wrongdoing. They might be shown to be unstable individuals, themselves the victims of emotional in-
security, and it might well be said of most of them that
they are unfit to be parents. They are part of that vicious
circle of maladjusted and unhappy parents rearing maladjusted and unhappy children. But they violate no law
on the statute books by being what they are, and futile
gestures to coerce them can but result in increasing the
child's shame and confusion. The time for educating
fathers and mothers in the responsibilities of parenthood
is usually long past when their children are brought into
court.

Children who are genuinely loved and cherished by
their parents seldom need to be brought into court. In
the parent's love, in the emotional security that develops
when a child knows himself to be loved and wanted, we
have a therapeutic measure which transcends any treatment that the court could prescribe. All authorities on
child welfare agree that what a child most needs from
birth to adolescence is the feeling of emotional security
that comes from parental love and understanding. Affection more than any other one thing establishes a child's
basic security.

A child may be considered "underprivileged" in relation to the material things of life, but no matter how poor
and ill-kept his home may be, if he feels that he belongs
there and that he can depend on his father and mother
to be "on his side" no matter what happens—if he knows
that while they may condemn what he has done, they will
never condemn him—such a child may unwittingly get
into trouble, but he will learn to control his behavior so

as not to distress those who love him and risk losing that love.

The same thing may be said of religious faith. The child who has learned to love God and who believes in God's infinite love for him will rarely be found among those classified as "juvenile delinquents." Like all children, he may occasionally stray from the narrow path of virtue, but he will not remain away any more than will the child who has impetuously run away from a good home. He will return to what he believes is right.

We wish that we could say that all children who have religious instruction are inspired with faith in the degree necessary to make it the guiding force of their lives. But the child of today is growing up in a materialistic world where the values by which people live make them want more and more of the material things of life. This atmosphere exerts a strong pressure upon the lives of our youth and makes it difficult to give them a true conception of spiritual values.

Another difficulty that has been encountered by preventive justice involves the matter of procedure. It was agreed at the beginning that hearings should be informal and private and that the terminology of criminal proceedings should be avoided. Cases involving children are initiated, not by an affidavit or information, but by a petition, which is not entitled "The State" versus the child, but is usually labelled "In Re" the child. There is no "charge" against the child, and he is not "convicted" or "found guilty" of any offense, nor is he "sentenced" to an institution or to probation.

Out of anxiety lest undesirable practices and procedures of the criminal court should permeate the juvenile court, ardent and sincere friends of the court insisted that all rules of evidence should also be eliminated. It is now being realized that, although proceedings in the juvenile court do not establish a criminal record against the child, and even though the purpose of the court is protective rather than punitive, it is a court, nevertheless, with the powers and prerogatives of a court. Men have always found that there must be safeguards against power, no matter how benevolently that power is exercised. Since parents and children will sometimes disagree with the court as to what is for the best interest of the child, it is essential that there should be a fair hearing to determine if the court is justified in taking over the function of the parents. It is all very well to say that the court is concerned with the offender and not with the offense, but it is also important to preserve the child's faith in justice and not give him cause to feel he is the victim of injustice. Young people have a keen sense of justice. They often become embittered as a result of their first experience with law and justice.

Technicalities and formalities can and should be eliminated, but justice—even preventive justice—should not be based on presumptions and implications or on confidential information supplied on condition that the source not be revealed. The child and his parents are entitled to see how and why he is adjudicated a delinquent, and it is incumbent on the court to recognize and enforce these rights.

I have had the opportunity to see justice administered by purely administrative agencies in Norway, Sweden, and Denmark. In those countries, Welfare Councils and Welfare Committees function in very much the same way that some of the interested authorities at one time felt would be desirable for the juvenile courts of this country. These committees are composed of representative citizens who serve as a matter of duty and without compensation. In this respect they may be compared with our draft boards. This might suggest the possibility of our adopting a similar system. But our draft boards do not have the amount of discretion which must be granted to those who determine the nature and extent of a child's maladjustment, and they have no responsibility for implementing their decisions. Our public welfare departments and public and private welfare agencies frequently have to rely on the court for authority to carry out their programs for dependent children. This indicates that relegation of juvenile court functions to a purely administrative agency or committee may not be feasible in our country.

Whatever the reason for occasional failure of many so-called "modern" methods of dealing with delinquency, no one who has seen the frightened face of a child behind bars would think of suggesting that we return to the old practice of trying children in criminal courts and incarcerating them in jails and penitentiaries. People impatient about the results thus far achieved by juvenile courts should remember that, while older generations have always bewailed the waywardness of youth, genuine public concern for the welfare of children is a comparatively recent development. Just a little over a hundred years ago Dickens wrote about the pitiable condition of children like Oliver Twist. The juvenile court movement itself has just passed the half-century mark. Child guidance clinics, youth centers, and many of our other youth programs are of such recent origin that they may be considered still in the experimental stage. We have extensive research projects trying to determine the causes and

cure of cancer, heart disease, and many other physical
and mental ills. But up to the present time, there has
been comparatively little intensive study and research
into the needs of youth and the causes of juvenile maladjustment.

In spite of all its shortcomings and difficulties, the Juvenile Court continues to exist. The highest courts of
most of our states have recognized the philosophy on
which juvenile courts are founded, and they have held
them to be constitutional on the grounds that their purpose is to protect and not to punish. In *Commonwealth
v. Fisher,* 62 Atlantic 198, which is one of the leading and
most often cited cases on this subject, the Supreme Court
of Pennsylvania held that, "To save a child from becoming
a criminal the Legislature may surely provide for the
salvation of such child by bringing it into one of the
courts of the state for the purpose of subjecting it to the
state's guardianship and protection," and that, "one of
the most important duties that society owes to its helpless members is performed in the measure that the law
is framed with wisdom and is carefully administered."

Although the general public may not yet have grasped
the full significance of the philosophy upon which the
court is based, it is the consensus that progress, if sometimes a little slow, is continuous and that the future of
the court looks promising. The judges of the juvenile
courts have contributed notably to their development.
Certainly they have carried on with faith and hope, doing
the best they can with the facilities they have and making
use of any other facilities which were available to them.
They have also exercised leadership in working towards
removal of environmental causes of delinquency and in
attempting to bring about coordination of the efforts of

the many institutions and agencies which serve the youth
of the nation. Looking backward along the path of progress, Dean Roscoe Pound said on the occasion of the fif-
tieth anniversary of the juvenile court:

As it was in the beginning, we saw only the individual child.
We sought to do for the individual child what normal house-
holds had done in the everyday conduct of the family. Later
we came to see that the delinquent child with whom the
juvenile court had to do was the product of conditions which
had operated to bring about his delinquency long before he
came to court, and that we had a preventive no less or even
more than a correctional task. We had not merely to adjust
or readjust the individual, but to deal with conditions which
were making for maladjustment of so many of his kind. In
other words, the Juvenile Court was not enough. It had to
be put in a setting of institutions doing more than the salvage
of individual children. But after this was perceived the difficulty was that we had hardly yet perfected the court for
the purposes for which we had set it up. Too few of our
courts, in the country as a whole, have even now the facilities and equipment for what we have demanded of them.
In the last few years, however, more and more we are seeking to organize comprehensive prevention, not for the locality
merely, but for the state, and to bring all agencies and programs of prevention into effective relation.